Coding Games in Scratch

A Step-by-Step Guide to Learn Coding Skills, Creating Own Games and Artificial Intelligence for Beginners & Kids

Written By Nicholas Ayden

Table Of Contents

Introduction

Both programming and coding are important in the world of computing and technology. The programming is the instrument that allows the execution of the automated tasks of a computer system so that the computer programs work in a certain way. We can say that it is the formal computer language that can be used to define a sequence of instructions for processing by a computer. However, coding is the process by which instructions are given to the computer using programming languages.

If you are oblivious to the computer world it can be difficult to understand coding, even the simplest details about coding may seem like an enigma. Once the algorithms of an application have been designed, the coding phase can begin. At this stage these algorithms have to be translated into a specific programming language; that is, the actions defined in the algorithms must be converted to instructions.

The logic of a program establishes what its actions are and in what order they should be executed. Therefore, it is convenient for every programmer to learn to design algorithms before moving on to the coding phase.

However, in this eBook, we will stay only on coding. From the beginning to the end, you will learn: What is Code? Loops, Variables, Advanced Topics, Artificial Intelligence: Machine Learning, etc.

Therefore, we recommend you continue reading chapter by chapter. You will find in each one, examples and exercises that will help you expand your knowledge in coding.

Enjoy it!!!

Chapter 1: What is Code?

Coding is the process of putting together the segments of your data that seem to illustrate an idea or concept (represented in your project as nodes). In this way, coding is a way of making abstractions from the existing data in their resources to build a greater understanding of the forces involved.

In NVivo, coding involves identifying references to the different ideas, concepts or categories of its resources and linking them to the nodes that represent them.

Remember that it is possible to code any portion of the content of a resource on any number of nodes to show that it is related to each of its concepts or categories.

Why do you need to code your resources?

The coding of the content of your resources can contribute significantly to your analysis in several ways:

- Coding generates ideas while codifying the material of its resources. It is possible to interpret passages and discover new meanings in the data.
- Coding allows you to gather and view all the material related to a category or case through all its resources. Viewing all this material allows you to review the coded segments in context and create new and more refined categories as you gain a new understanding of the meaning of the data.
- The codification of its resources facilitates the search for patterns and theories. It is possible to browse the encoded content of your resources using queries and search functionality to test theories and find new patterns in your data.

Example: When coding in C the algorithm of the program Add, seen in the previous section (Design), something similar to:

```
#include <stdio.h>



int main ()

{

   int a, b, c;



   printf ("\ n first n% number (integer):", 163);

   scanf ("% d", & a);

   printf ("\ n second n% number (integer):", 163);

   scanf ("% d", & b);

   c = a + b;

   printf ("\ n The sum is:% d", c);
```

```
return 0;
```

To encode an algorithm you have to know the syntax of the language to which it will be translated. However, regardless of the programming language in which a program is written, it will be its algorithm that determines its logic. The logic of a program establishes what its actions are and in what order they should be executed. Therefore, it is convenient for every programmer to learn to design algorithms before moving on to the coding phase.

Programming languages

A programming language can be defined as an artificial language that allows you to write the instructions of a computer program, or put another way. A programming language allows the programmer to communicate with the computer to tell it what it has to do. Many programming languages have invented by man. We can classify into three main types: **the machine**, **low level**, and **high level**.

Machine language is the only one that understands the digital computer. it is its "natural language". Only two symbols can be used on it: zero (0) and one (1). Therefore, machine language is also called binary language. The computer can only work with bits. However, it is not easy for the programmer to write instructions such as:

```
10100010

11110011

00100010

00010010
```

For this reason, more understandable programming languages were invented for the programmer.

Thus, **low-level** languages appeared, also called assembly languages, which allow the programmer to write the instructions of a program using English abbreviations, also called mnemonic words, such as: ADD, DIV, SUB, etc., instead of use zeros and ones. For example, the instruction:

```
ADD a, b, c
```

It could be the translation of the action:

$$c \leftarrow a + b$$

This action is present in the Add algorithm of the previous section (Design), which indicated that in the memory space represented by the variable c the sum of the two numbers stored in the memory spaces represented by the variables a and b must be stored.

A program written in an assembly language has the disadvantage that it is not understandable to the computer since it is not composed of zeros and ones. To translate the instructions of a program written in an assembly language to instructions of a machine language, you must use a program called assembler, as shown in the following figure:

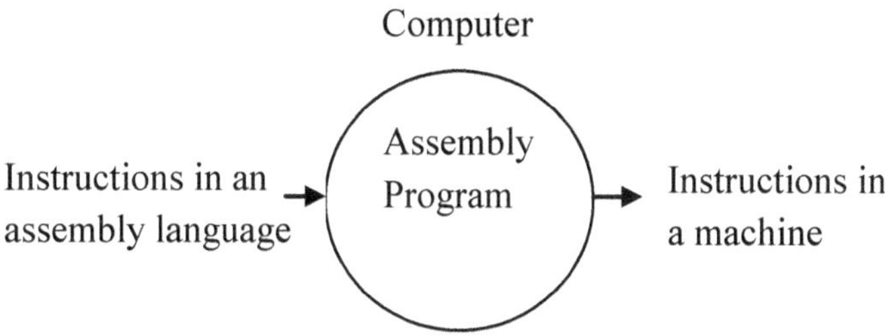

An added difficulty to binary languages is the fact that they are dependent on the machine, or rather, the processor, that is, each processor uses a different machine language, a different set of instructions, which is defined in its hardware. Consequently, a program written for a type of processor cannot be used on other equipment that uses a different processor, since the program will not be portable. For this program to work on a second computer, all instructions written in the machine language of the first computer must be translated into the binary language of the second computer, which is a very expensive and complex job for the programmer.

Likewise, since the instructions that can be written in an assembly language are always associated with the binary instructions of a particular computer, assembly languages are also processor dependent. However, high-level languages are independent of the processor, that is, a program written on any computer with high-level language can be transported to any other computer, with small changes or even none.

A high-level language allows the programmer to write the instructions of a program using words or syntactic expressions. For example, in C you can use words such as case, if, for, while, etc. to build with the instructions like:

```
if (nº> 0) printf ("The number% is positive", 163);
```

Which translated into Spanish comes to say that, if number is greater than zero, then write the message on the screen: "The number is positive."

If words in other languages of very easy compression can be used for the programmer, we can say that those languages are considered high-level. In contrast, low-level languages are those that are closer to the "understanding" of the machine. Other high-level languages are: Ada, BASIC, COBOL, FORTRAN, Pascal, etc.

Another important feature of high-level languages is that, for most of the instructions in these languages, several instructions in an assembly language would be needed to indicate the same. In the same way that, most of the instructions of an assembly language, also groups several instructions of a machine language.

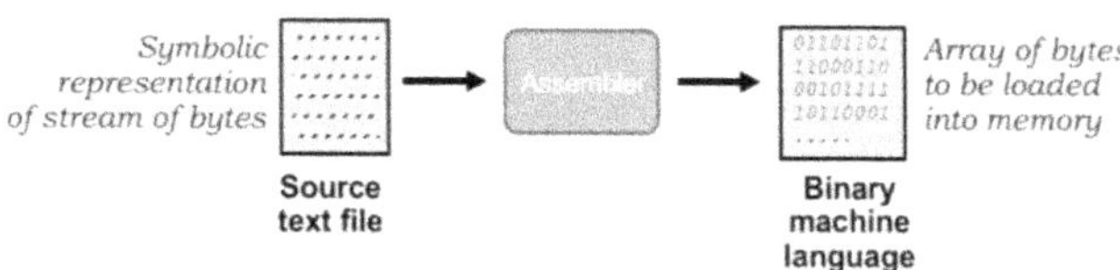

- Abstracts bit-level representation of instructions and addresses
- We'll learn UASM ("microassembler"), built into BSim
- Main elements:
  - Values
  - Symbols
  - (symbols for addresses)
  - Macros

On the other hand, a program written in a high-level language also does not get rid of the inconvenience of the fact that it is not understandable to the computer and, therefore, to translate the instructions of a program written in a high-level language to instructions of a machine language, you have to use another program that, in this case, is called a compiler.

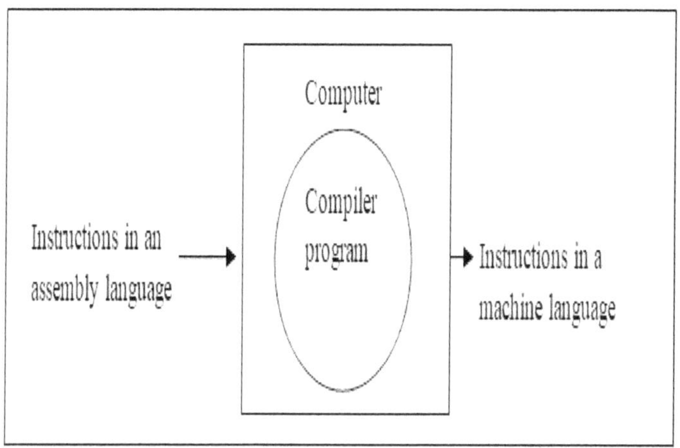

Compilers and interpreters

The instruction set written in a high-level language is called the source code of the program. Thus, the compiler is a program that receives as input data the source code of a program written by a programmer and generates as output a set of instructions written in the binary language of the computer where they will be executed. The set of instructions generated by the compiler is called the object code of the program, also known as machine code or binary code, since it is, in itself, a program executable by the machine.

Normally, a C programmer will use an editing program to write the source code of a program, and save it in a file with the extension (.c); for example, "Add.c". Next, a C compiler will translate the source code into object code, saving it with another extension, which, depending on the operating system may vary. For example, in Windows, it will be saved with the extension (.obj), short for the object.

On the other hand, there is a type of program called interpreter, which also serves to translate the source code of a program into object code, but its way of acting is different from that of a compiler.

The operation of an interpreter is characterized by translating and executing, one by one, the instructions of the source code of a program, but without generating as output object code. The process performed by an interpreter is as follows: read the first instruction of the source code, translate it into object code and execute it; then do the same with the second instruction; and so on, until you reach the last instruction of the program, as long as there is no error that stops the process. In a program, there can be three types of errors: syntax, execution, and logic.

Types of errors

When a syntax error exists in any instruction of the source code of a program, this error will prevent both the compiler and the interpreter from translating said instruction, since neither of them will understand what the programmer is telling you. For example, if instead of the instruction:

```
printf ("\ n first n% number (integer):", 163);
```

A programmer writes:

```
prrintf ("\ n first n% number (integer):", 163);
```

When the compiler or the interpreter reads this line of code, neither of them will understand what prrintf is and, therefore, they will not know how to translate this instruction into machine code, therefore, both will stop the translation and notify the programmer with a message of error.

In summary, syntax errors are detected in the process of translating the source code into binary code. On the contrary that it happens with the errors of execution and of logic that can only be detected when the program is running.

A runtime error occurs when the computer cannot execute any instruction correctly. For example, the instruction:

```
c = 5/0;
```

It is syntactically correct and will be translated into binary code. However, when the computer tries to perform the division:

```
5/0
```

An execution error will occur, since, mathematically, it cannot be divided by zero.

As for logic errors, they are the most difficult to detect. When a program has no syntax or execution errors, but still does not work well, this is due to the existence of some logical error. So, a logic error occurs when the results obtained are not as expected. For example, if instead of the instruction:

```
c = a + b;
```

A programmer would have written:

```
c = a * b;
```

Until the result of the operation was shown on the screen, the programmer could not realize the error, provided he already knew the result of the sum in advance. In this case, the programmer could easily notice the error, but, when the operations are more complex, the logic errors can be very difficult to detect.

Sequence

- All scripts are encoding, but not all encodings are scripts.
- The coding includes more than just scripting, but scripting is one soort coding
- Examples of tasks where scripts can automate a website are:
- A chatbot that returns texts.
- A pop-up window or -form will appear on the screen in response to user behavior.
- To make an animation when a visitor moves beyond a certain point on the page.
- Fill a page after a search action on a site.

- By logging into a website with username and password.

What can you make with code?

You can do many things with codes. For example, let's see what can be done with JavaScript code.

The things that can be done with Code are very varied, among the most prominent are:

1. You can obtain the information about the browser that the user is using, the version of it, the operating system on which it is running and even the screen resolution that you have configured on your computer.

2. You can work with pop-up and interactive dialogs created with div elements, instead of pop-up windows, which have stopped being used for security and design reasons.

3. You can create sophisticated menu systems with pop-up submenus that are activated with the user action.

4. Values entered in form fields can be validated before they are sent to the server.

5. You can create navigation trees to make it easier for users to move from one page to another through your website.

6. You can create substitution effects for images controlled by the action of placing or removing the mouse pointer.

7. You can create some animations such as transitions of images and objects from a web page.

8. You can change the position of HTML elements on the web page dynamically or controlled by the movement of the mouse pointer.

9. You can redirect the user from one page to another, without the need for a static link.

10. You can perform some calculations with the values entered in the form fields.

11. You can get the date of the operating system where the web page is running on the client.

12. Sophisticated calendar controls can be created to select a date, instead of being manually entered by users in form fields.

What is scratch?

Scratch is a graphic programming environment developed by a group of researchers from the Lifelong Kindergarten Group of the MIT Media Laboratory, under the direction of Dr. Mitchel Resnick.

This graphic environment makes programming more attractive and accessible for anyone who faces for the first time to learn a programming language. According to its creators, it was designed as a means of expression to help children and young people express their ideas creatively while developing logical thinking skills.

Scratch allows you to easily create your own interactive stories, animations, games, record sounds and make artistic creations.

The application of block programming languages allows a visual presentation of the paradigm and methodology of computer programming allowing to focus on the logic of programming leaving aside the syntax of programming languages (semicolons, parentheses, etc.).

Scratch, the programming language

It is a visual programming language, oriented to the teaching of block programming to children, without having to delve deeply into the development of the code.

It is a project created by MIT, launched in 2005, free and open-source; available for Windows, Mac, and Linux.

Scratching is an English term that means reusing code, and that means that the program allows you to use internal resources and modify them to the user's liking.

Characteristics and virtues

- You can handle it online or offline. The good thing about the first is that it is always updated, making the user experience never stop improving. Here you can download the software, in case you want to use it on a computer without an Internet connection.

- The Scratch programming language works with blocks, where the user places some bricks with certain conditions, which make the object move to one side or the other.

- It is a collaborative environment, where each user can participate in several projects, moving blocks and interacting with the object.

- Those same blocks are classified by colors, making operation even more intuitive.

- Based on the Logo programming language, developed by Danny Bobrow, among others.

- It is usually recommended for children between 6 and 16 years old, but as we said, it can be used by anyone who wants, without any type of cutter.
- Programs can be launched directly from a web page.
- Autonomous Learning.
- Benefits of this programming language:
- Free, free software.
- Ideal for taking the first steps in the world of code.
- Available in several formats: offline (download on Windows, Mac, and Linux), and online.
- Once the project is finished, it can be downloaded and shared on the internet.
- You can use it in many languages.

- With the Scratch programming language, you learn to program without typing code.
- Transmits to the child the need to solve problems in an orderly manner.
- Being a scalable learning method, a problem can always be further developed, increasing the level of the challenge, and consequently, expanding the creative ability of the student.
- Depth of mathematical concepts: coordinates, algorithms, variables, or randomness, among others.
- Develop the capacity of self-criticism, doubting any hypothetical solution.

Scratch, the code editor

The Scratch editor divides the screen into several panels: on the left are the stage and the list of objects, in the middle are the block palettes and on the right the program, costumes and sounds editor. The block palette contains a series of blocks that can be dragged and dropped in the Programs area to build the scripts that constitute our project. The block palette is divided into ten groups of blocks: Motion, Appearance, Sound, Pencil, Data, Events, Control, Sensors, Operators, and More Blocks (to create special blocks and other extensions).

Let's go by parts!

- Contents
- The objects
- Information about an Object
- The costumes
- The sounds
- The programs
- The blocks
- Stage
- Top bar

The objects

The Objects area can manage the objects or characters that we have been adding to the program. We can select the object we want to edit or add a new object:

Both from the gallery of Scratch characters, and drawing a new one, uploading a photo that we have on our computer or taking a photo if we have a webcam installed:

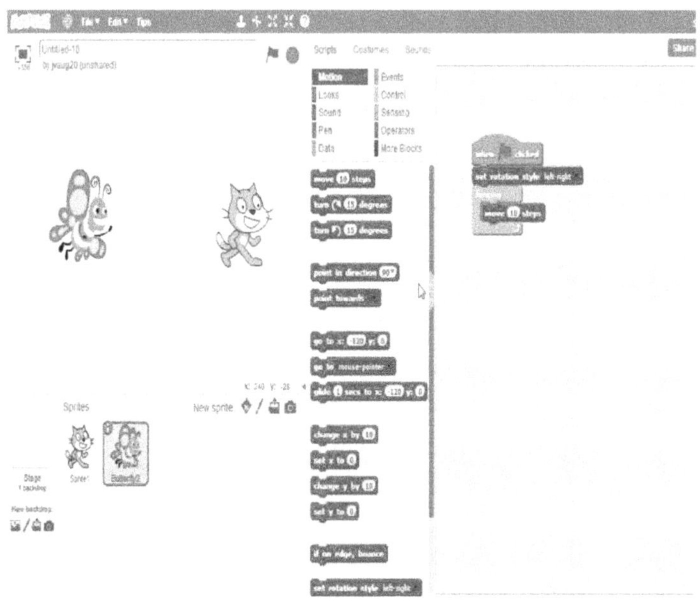

Information about an Object

By clicking on the blue i in the upper corner of the object we can access the information panel of that object being able to edit among other things the name of the object.

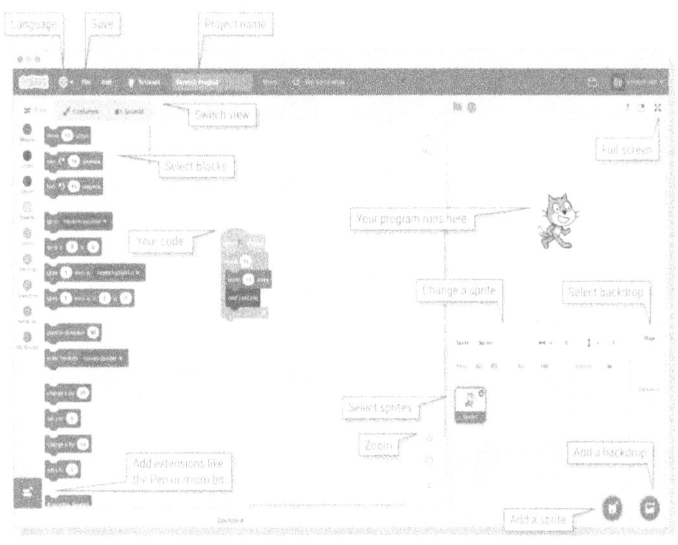

The costumes

In the area of costumes we can add or draw different images for our characters as well as edit them. With the program we can control with what costume the character will be shown on stage.

The sounds

It allows you to add or edit sounds to our characters, both from the Scratch sound gallery and from files that we have on our computer.

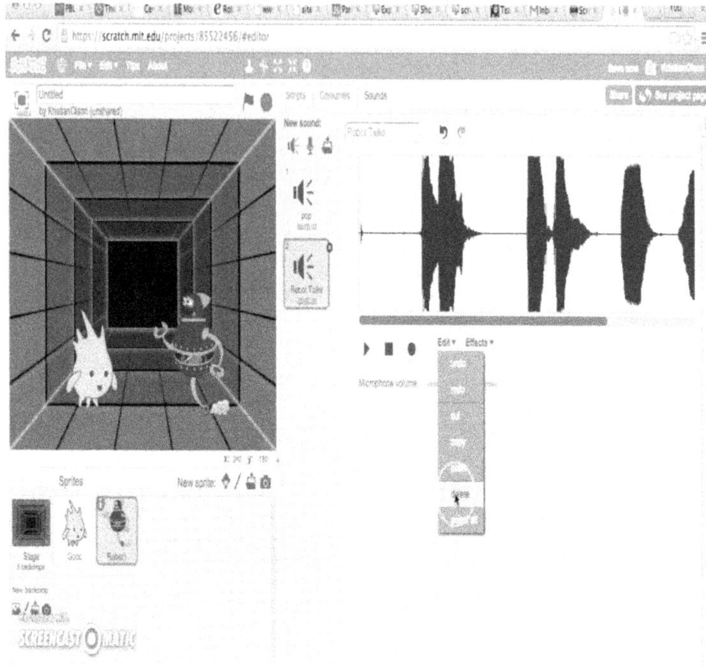

The programs

The Programs tab contains the instruction blocks assembled so that they give life to our object.

From the block area you can drag and drop the different blocks to the Programs area where they can be assembled together forming the programs of our project.

Each of the objects in the Object area, including the scenario, has its own programs that control only that particular object.

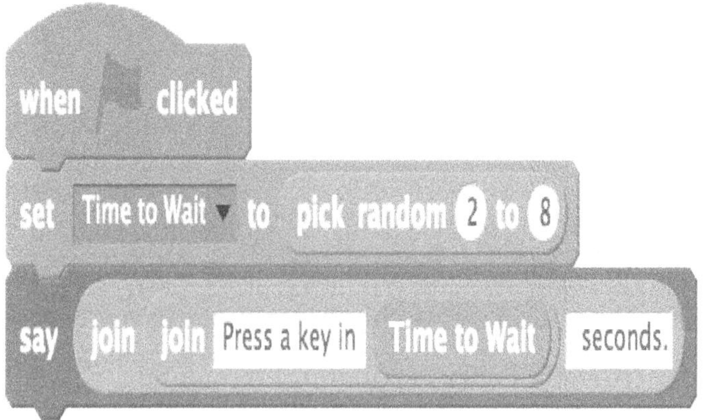

The blocks

The block palette contains a series of blocks that can be dragged and dropped in the Programs area to build the scripts that constitute our project. The block palette is divided into ten groups of blocks: Motion, Appearance, Sound, Pencil, Data, Events, Control, Sensors, Operators, and More Blocks (to create special blocks and other extensions).

Stage

The scenario is a type of object that represents the background of the screen and is the place where all other objects interact.

As an object: that Programs, Costumes and Sounds can be added in a similar way to other objects.

As a place: where the rest of the objects interact, it represents a coordinate system where the center would be the point 0.0 (x = 0, y = 0) where the x correspond to the horizontal position and the y to the vertical position.

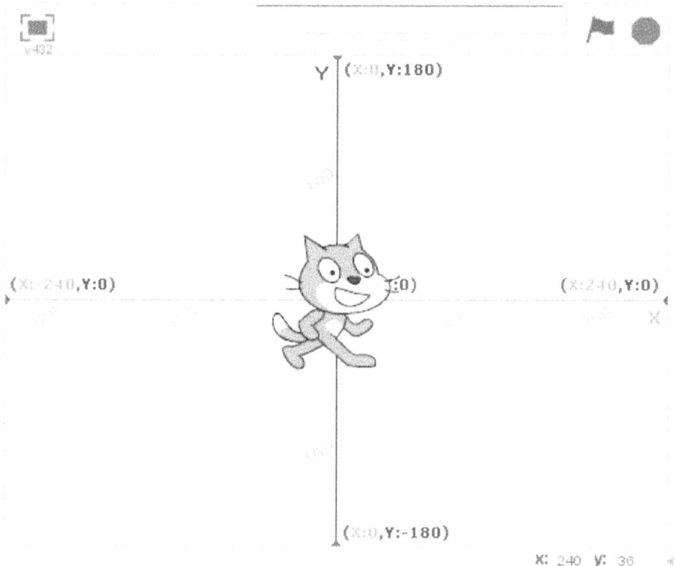

Top bar

Scratch button

Allows you to exit and return to the main page of the Scratch website

Menu file

<u>*New*</u>: Create a new blank project.

<u>*Save now*</u>: save the project in its current state

Save a copy: Create a copy of the current project to modify it.

Go to My Stuff: Link to the My Stuff section, where all your projects are.

Upload from your computer: Upload .sb2 projects you have saved.

Download to your computer: download the current project in .sb2 format

Revert: returns the project to its initial state before opening it the last time.

Edit menu

Undelete – Its function is to undo a sprite, costume, sound, or script that was recently deleted.

Small stage layout – Its funtion is to make the stage shrink to a s not a big size, i.e., a maller size.

Turbo Mode – It is where the code is executed very quickly. It is for setting the player into Turbo Mode.

Edit Buttons

Below you can find 4 buttons with which you can edit the Objects or Programs.

Duplicate: allows you to create a copy of the object or program we stamp

Cut: allows you to cut and eliminate the object or program in which we put the scissors.

Expand: allows you to enlarge the size of an object on the stage

Reduce: allows you to reduce the size of an object on the stage

Help: open the description, in English, of a block in the help section.

Building & Running a Script

As far as, Scratch will run one block from every script each tick. Let's say you had these scripts:

As soon as you click the green flag, the program will run the first block of the first script (go to 0, 0). Scratch will find the next running script (the second one) and run the first block there. So, loops such as forever and repeat count as blocks, so nothing would happen, except that the loop would start.

What scratch is going to do is to go back to the first script and check the next block (forever) and run that (again doing nothing). So, it will move to the next running script and run the other block, the next, in this case, in line (turn 25 degrees).

Look that, it will jump back to first script and move 10 steps, then go to script 2 and turn 25 degrees. And, there will be a continuity of alternative between moving and turning for the rest of the project.

The tricky part is that the order in which scripts are run (which is run first, the one with the moving block or the turn block?) is difficult to pin down. Keep in mind that, in scratch, it's up to you to place scripts wherever you would like them go first. That means, basically, the scripts run from the top to the bottom, with no concern for their x location.

So, one more time, the complications of the things get worse. You have to know which sprite you will fire first when there are multiple sprites involved.

Important: Make sure to not confuse sin the custom blocks with "run without screen refresh" checked are treated as just one block in the execution order.

Fortunately, the users who program in this way (rather than using, for example, broadcasts) are generally making projects simple enough that it doesn't matter the order in which events are fired.

Creating a Scratch account

Download and install directly from the project website: http://scratch.mit.edu/

In the zone "Download Scratch" we can find an installer for Windows and Mac. There are not yet specific packages for Linux (they indicate that they are working on it), but there are some instructions on how to make it work under different distributions of this system in the project forums.

In the first execution of the program, the environment is in English:

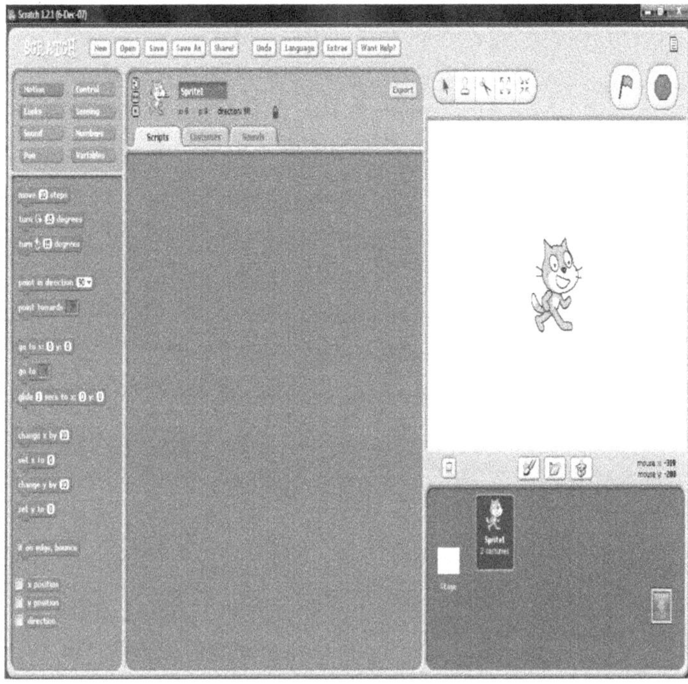

For switching the language, you just need to make a click on the "Language" button. Select "the language you want"...

Create an online account

How to access the Scratch website

1. Open your preferred search engine; Google, Yahoo, etc.

2. Type "Scratch" in the search bar

3. Select the first search result titled "Scratch - Imagine, Program, Share"

Language setting (optional)

4. Once the Scratch site has loaded, scroll to the bottom of the page

5. Search for the language selection drop-down menu and select your preferred language

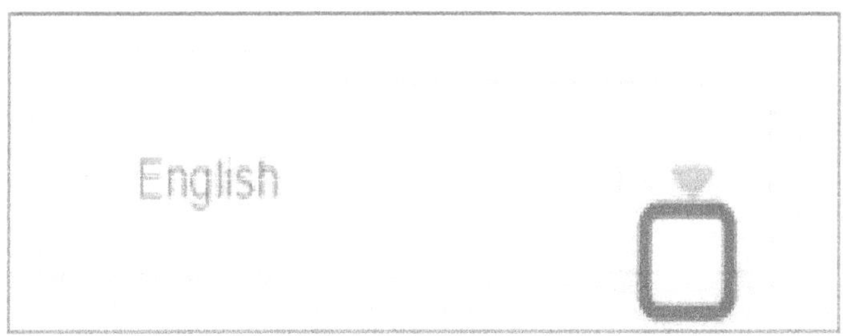

Creating and registering your account

In this step, you will begin to create your free account.

1. Look for the "Join Scratch" link in the upper right section of the website and click on it to start creating your account.

1. A new window will open and you will see several fields. Enter your preferred username in the first field.

2. The second and third fields are for your password. Enter the same simple password in both fields. It is recommended to insert a password with, at least 6 characters long

* Keep your username and password within reach and easily accessible.

Once you have finished entering your username and password, click on the "Next" button to continue.

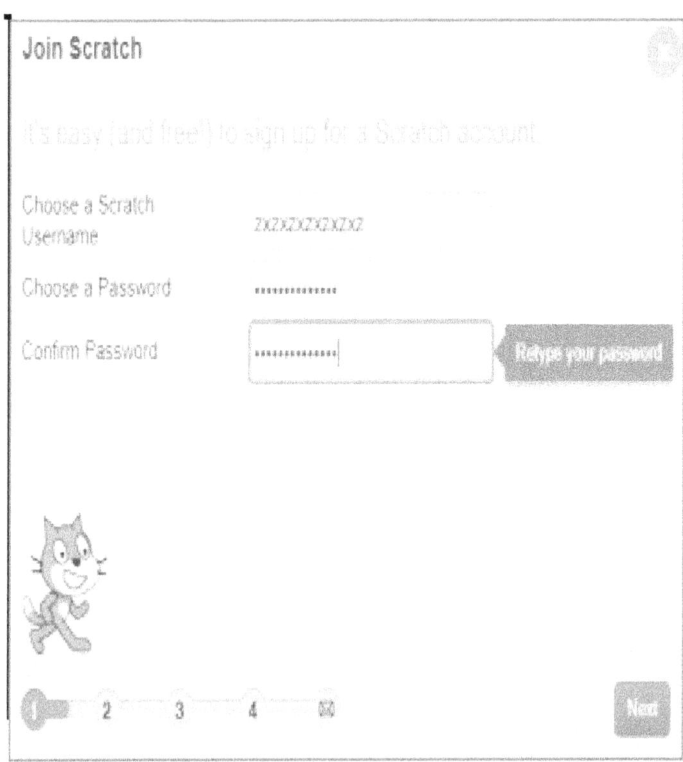

At this stage, you will continue to create your account and provide additional information to set up your account.

1. In the first field, enter your date of birth by selecting the month and year from the drop-down menu

2. Select your gender

3. From the drop-down menu, you can select your country residence.

4. When you finish entering the information, you can click on "Next" to go to the last stage

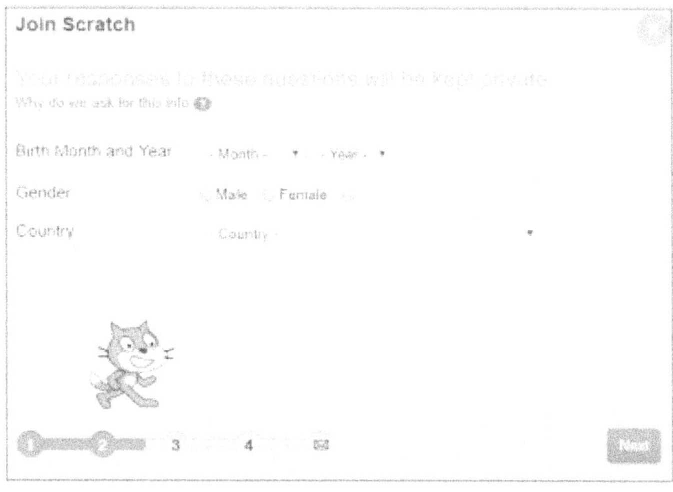

1. In the field: "email address", enter your parents' email.

2. The second field is the same; Confirm the email address by typing the same address as in the previous field.

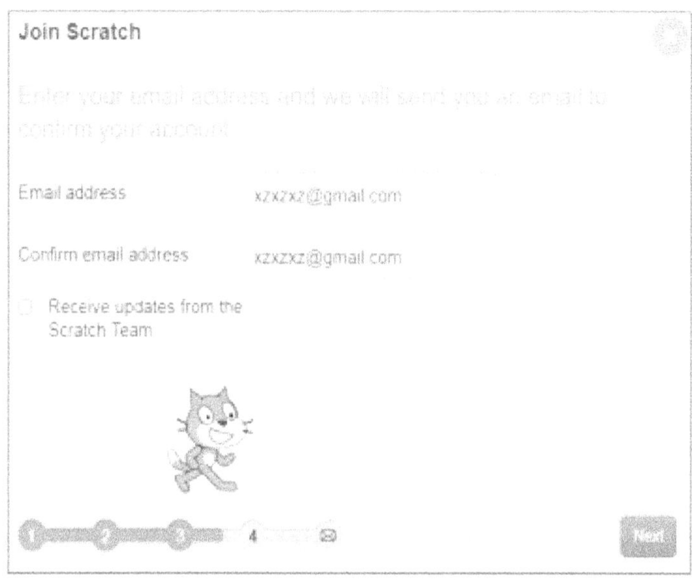

Congratulations! You have completed the registration process.

Press the "OK Lets GO!" button to complete the process.

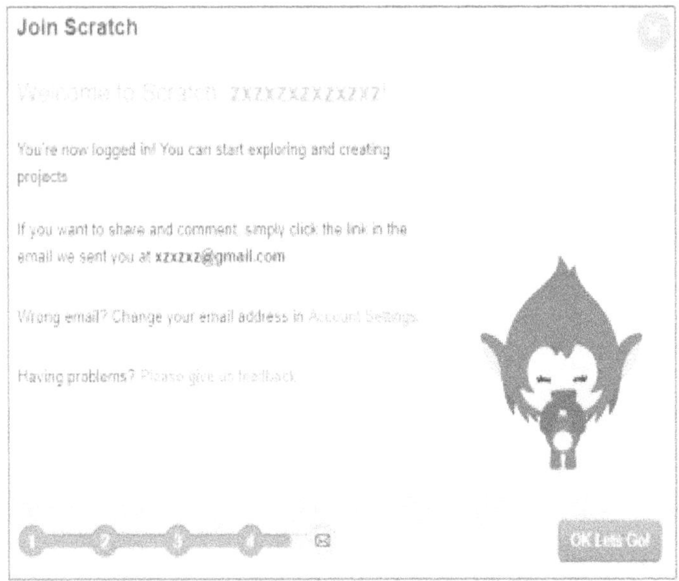

Confirmation email for your new Scratch account

Once the registration process is successful, an automatic email will be sent to your email address.

1. Open your email and look for the email sent by Scratch. It can be identified easily by looking for: "Confirm the email address of Scratch".

2. So, the text: "Confirm my email address" will appear in the email they will send you. Make a click on the button for final confirmation.

Greetings from the Scratch Team at MIT!

A few minutes ago, you requested to link this email address to the Scratch account **zxzxzxzxzxzxz**. Please confirm your email address by clicking the button below.

Chapter 2: Loops

Project #1: Dino Dance Battle

1. Open the Scratch program by accessing the Scratch website and entering your username and password.

2. Create a new project by clicking on Create and then on File-New

3. Insert a name to your project: Dino Dance Battle

4. By default the object (cat) appears. You will delete it to insert another different object. To do this, select the scissors from the toolbar and click on the cat. This will be deleted.

5. Next, select the scenario by clicking on the first icon of the toolbar that appears in the lower left of the screen

6. Choose the image called Spotlight-stage in the theme "Music and Dance" and press Ok

7. Delete the white background that comes by default and that appears in the central block of the screen. Erase it with scissors.

8. Now add the character (the dinosaur in this case). To do this you have to insert a new object by clicking on the first icon on the toolbar of the objects at the bottom of the screen

Adding Sound Effects

Select the Object and in sounds, click on import, select Jump.

Go to Sound and add: play Jump sound, below: by pressing the up arrow key. With this action you will hear the sound every time you jump. In this case, unlike the previous sound, you don't have to wait for the sound to end to execute the next instruction. This should be run almost at the same time to make it seem as real as possible.

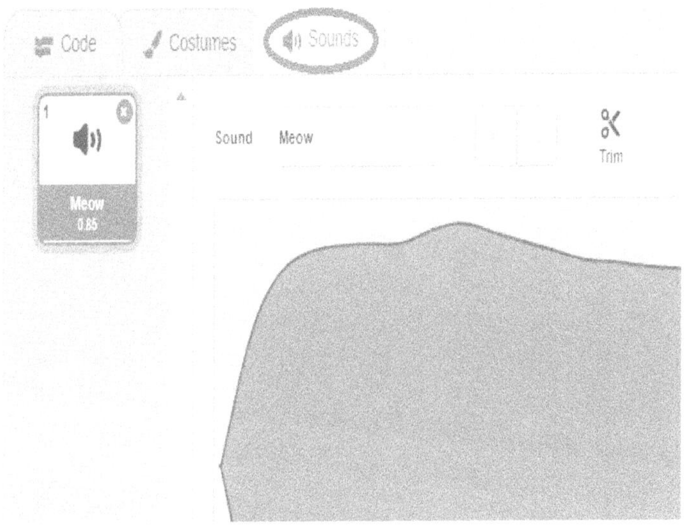

You can add default sounds in the program, using the instruction: play note 60 for 0.2 pulses, this instruction allows you to play a piano note for 0.2 pulses. This instruction can be added where desired, to simulate the sound of a step or crouch. An example below:

Let's import the music file

1. Click on the Sounds tab, and then click the Import button to display the Import Sound dialog box.
2. Browse to and select the music file you want to add. In this game, we will use the Drum sound from the Music Loops folder in Scratch's sound library. To do so, make a click on OK to add the new sound.
3. Click back to the Scripts tab and set the play sound block to use the new sound file.

4. Click the flag to play the game and listen to the music.

1. Enter the Scratch online page.

Click on the part that says My Stuff button near the top right of the web page.

Before doing anything, you must pay attention to all information on the far right. There, they will tell you which projects that have been shared. If the unshared button appears, it's a sign to aware you that that the project has been shared.

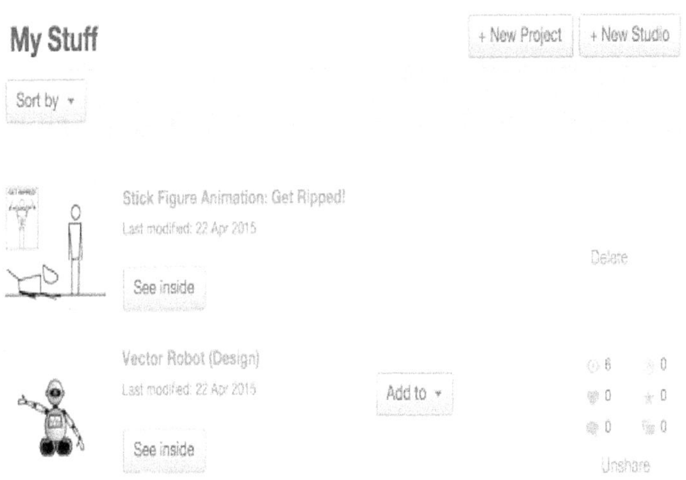

Click the title of the project to share.

Click the Share button.

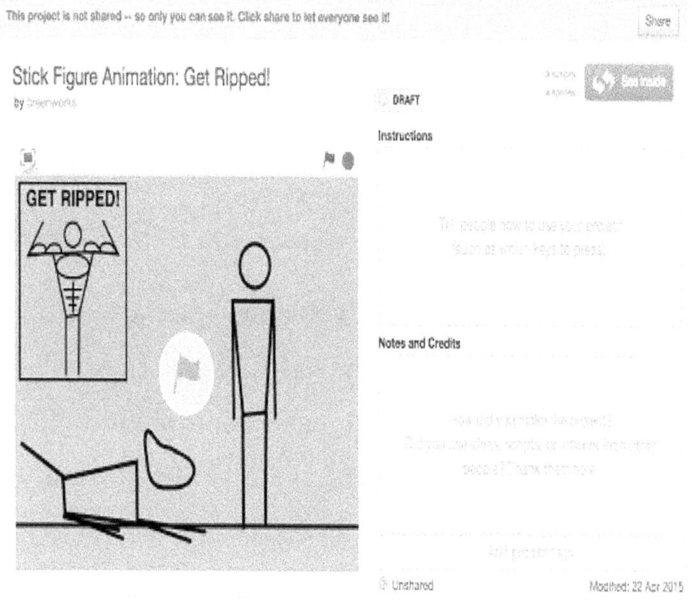

There are some instructions that are available that you have to fill them. You will find them the Instructions box and the Notes and Credits box and then add one to three tags.

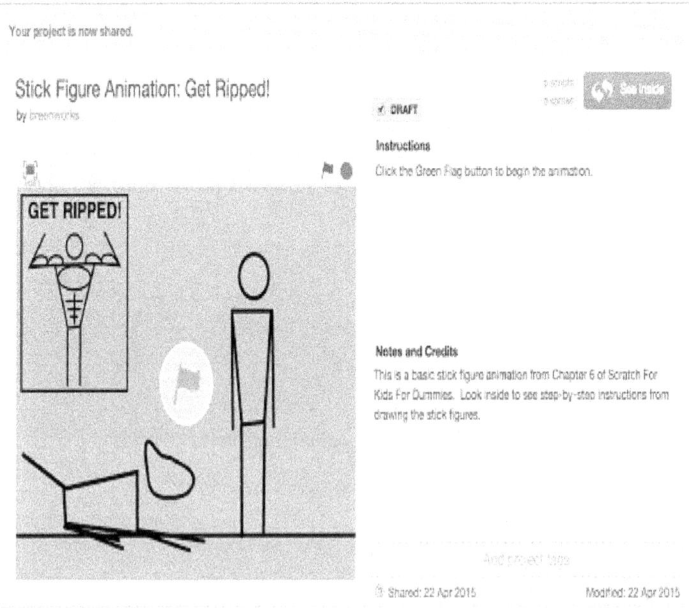

Sharing a project from the Scratch Offline Editor is easy. You just need to select the File menu and select Share to Website. You must log into your Scratch account and then follow Steps 2–6 previously mentioned above.

Chapter 3: Variables

A variable is a data structure referenced by a name that can change content during the execution of a program.

From the point of view of the Scratch user, we can create labels by assigning them a name, giving them an initial value and modifying the value during program execution. This label can be used to make calculations with operators or checks with control blocks.

What uses can we give to a variable?

We can do a lot of things with variables, for example:

- Store the number of successful questions in a quiz.
- Store the total points we have in a card game.
- Store the number of repetitions we carry in iteration.

Some examples:

Hello world

123

3.14

0

-321

true/false

{nothing - empty string}

Identifying Built-In Variables

Creating a variable is easy. You can use it by dragging in a block from the Data tab that looks like this:

Basketball Speed

To find many other blocks that are similar to the variable created, go the tab of blocks. Below, an example, in the Motion tab, there are three built-in variables:

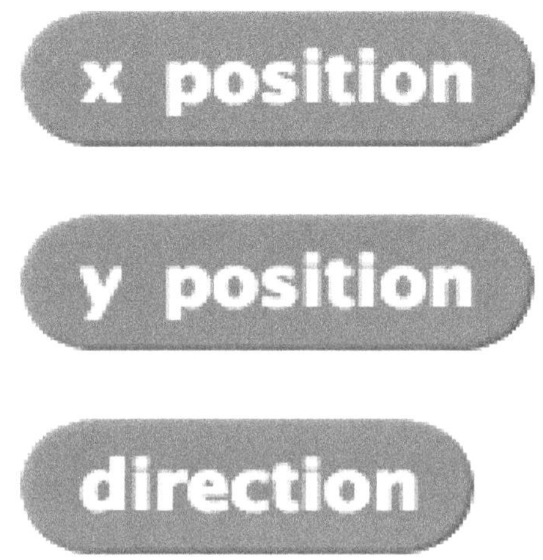

For this reason, in this section of our eBook, we will help you explore some of the built-in variables available in Scratch.

Tempo

Tempo variable is one of the built-in variables that this program allows you to use. You can find it in the Sound tab. Click on the check box the variable name in the Sound tab to display the temp on the stage. We can either set the tempo to a specific number of bpm (beats per minute), or change the tempo by some amount. Consider the code below:

```
when space key pressed
set tempo to 60 bpm
repeat 2
    play note 60 for 0.5 beats
    repeat 3
        play drum 11 for 0.25 beats
        change tempo by 20
```

Exercise

Can you find the value of tempo if you were to move the "change tempo by 20" block as shown?

```
when space key pressed
set tempo to 60 bpm
repeat 2
    play note 60 for 0.5 beats
    repeat 3
        play drum 11 for 0.25 beats
    change tempo by 20
```

Answer

You can get information from the user. There is a lot of information that Scratch gives us. You can find a useful "ask and wait" block in the Sensing tab. Reacting to the user input is easy. You just need to check if they entered a certain value. We will show you that in the script below as an example. Let's say Hello if the user enters the name Dan, and Go away! Otherwise!

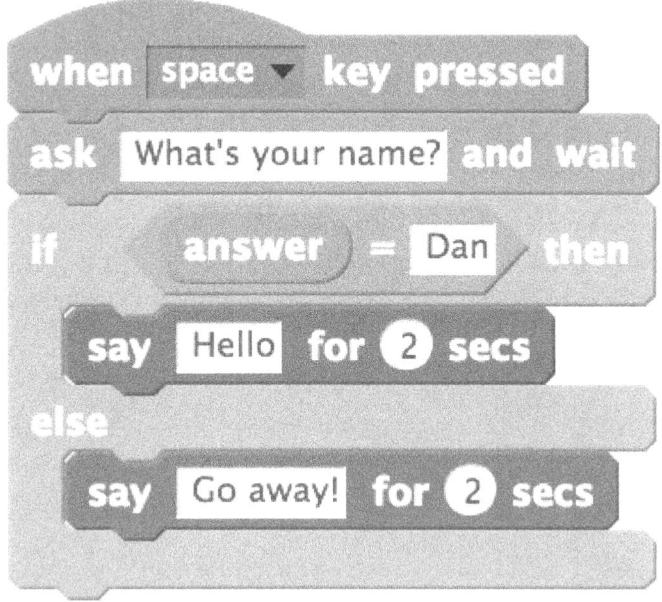

You can use "join block" to improve the script above, which you can find in the Operators tab. Join blocks facilitate you to squish two things together (often called concatenation in Computer Science parlance). If you use the join block as follows, we can say “Hello, Dan”, or “Go away, somebody”, where somebody will be whatever name the user entered.

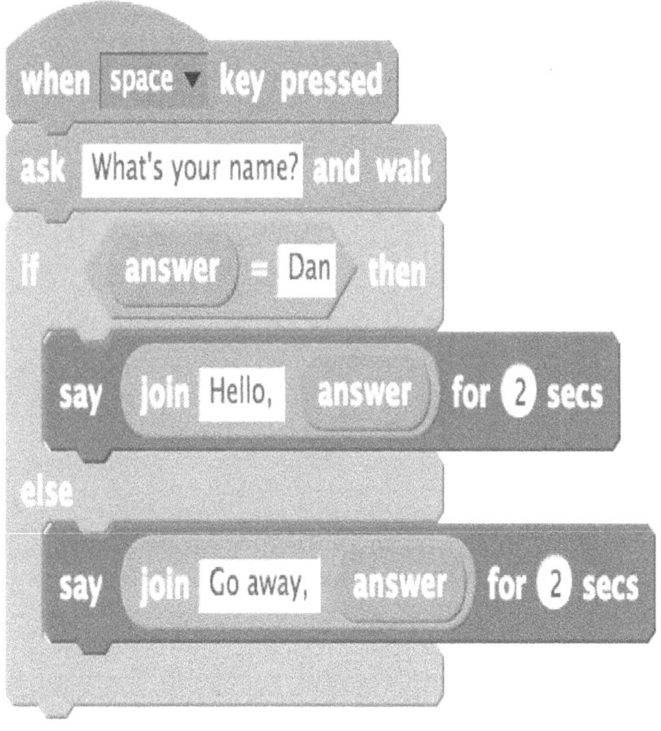

It is possible to allow more than one name to trigger the Hello message. What you need to do is use the "or block". You will find it in the Operators tab. Doing so, you will be able to check for more than one condition. Let's an example below to see how the script will say hello to either Dan or Zoe, but will say go away to anyone else.

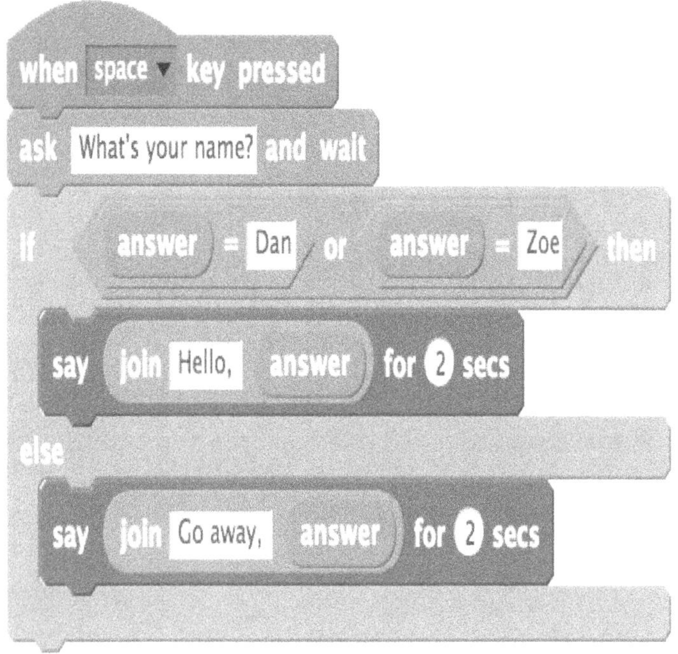

Let's create a simple game, in which the user has to try to press a key after a certain number of seconds. If the user is close, congratulate them. In case that the user is not close, say him to try again.

Let's say that we don't want the wait time to always be the same, for this, we will need to create a variable that we can use instead of a specific number. When the variable is created, the computer itself will pick a random number to use for the wait time. This will help the user understand how long he needs to wait.

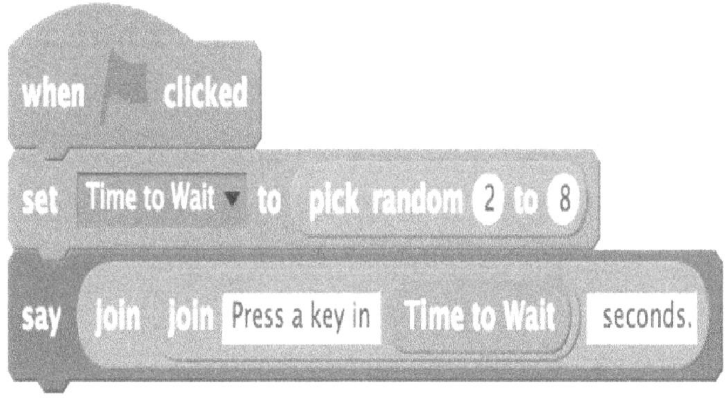

You must open the Sensing tab and make a click on the checkbox beside the timer variable to show the built-in timer variable on the stage. The timer on the stage in the final version of the game is not necessary. However, it can help while creating the game. It resets to 0 every time you click on the green flag. You can use "reset timer" block if you want to use something other than the flag being clicked. This will help you to begin the game to do so.

In order to determine if the user is “close enough” to the time to wait, we need to consider what happens if they are slightly above, or slightly below the wait time. Let’s say that the wait time was supposed to be 5 seconds. And, you just like the user to “win” if they press a key at intervals a second of the wait time. In case that the user presses the key a second too late, at 5.5 seconds, what we can do is to merely take off the timer value from the wait time:

5.5−5=0.5

Let’s imagine that the user presses the key half a second too soon, the same thing will happen. The difference will be a negative number:

4.5−5=−0.5

The ideal is simply asked if the time clicked is less than half a second away from what we expected. What we need to do this is to convert the negative answer below into a positive value. Using the absolute value operation we have learned in math class: We have

$|5.5-5|=0.5$

$|4.5-5|=0.5$

The same happen in Scratch. So, absolute value can be used to find the distance away, always positive. To do so, you can choose the absolute value operator in the Operators tab, though it will initially appear like below:

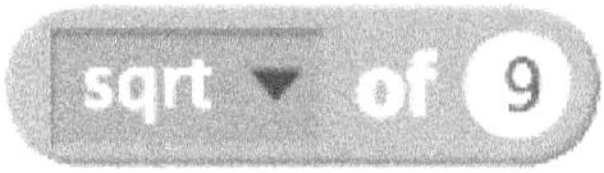

Using the above block, you must make a click on the sqrt, and select abs. It is short for absolute value. After doing so, you can generate code that perform when the user press a key. Check to see if

the user pressed a key within half a second before or after the expected wait time.

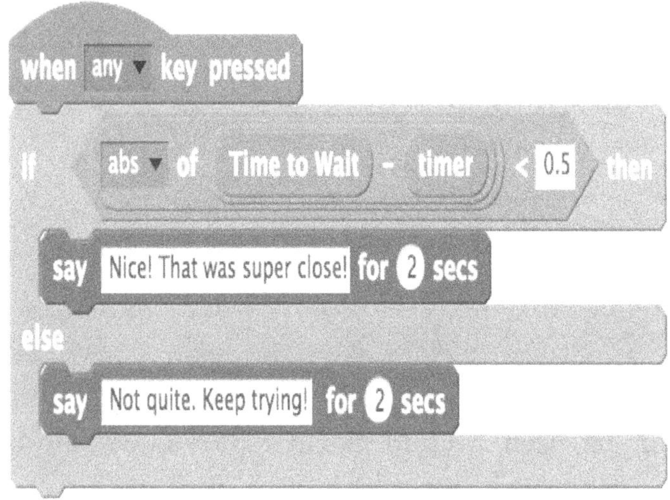

Project #2: Fish Clicker

The clickables

First, the project will need a clickable. It can easily be made by first picking a costume, and then creating the following script.

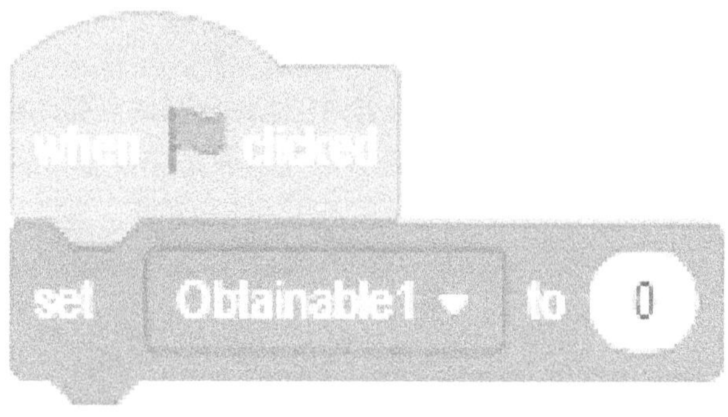

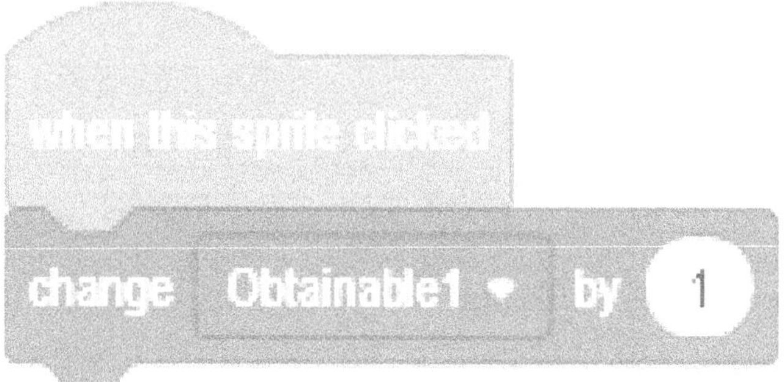

However, there is a flaw within that script. If building or upgrade to make the clicking power increase was created, the previous script wouldn't work.

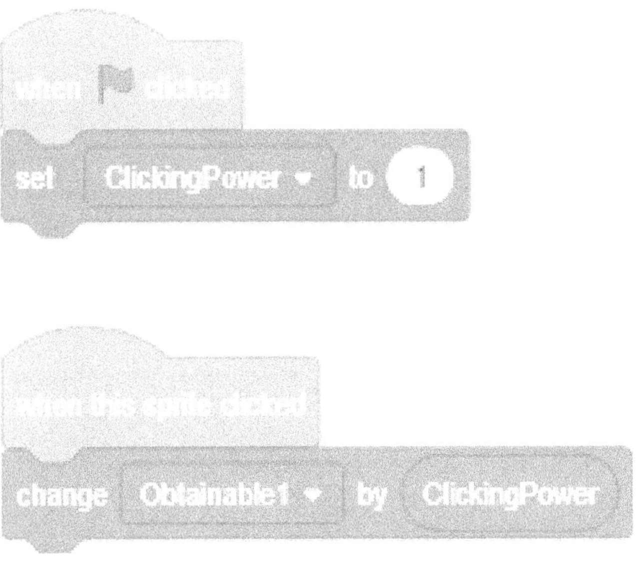

Buildings

To make the buildings, you must take a decision. Should the buildings to be shown next to the clickable or should they be shown after using a button. For the button, see Button Section.

Button Section

First make two costumes, one for entering shop and one for exiting.

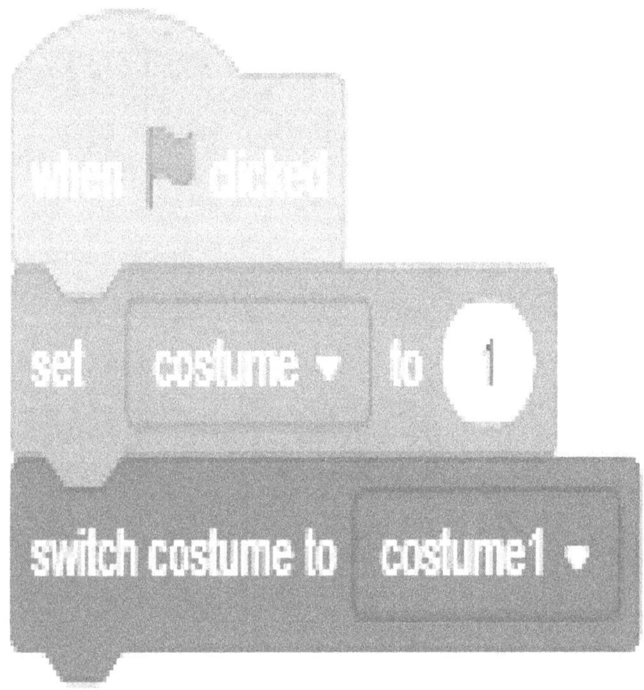

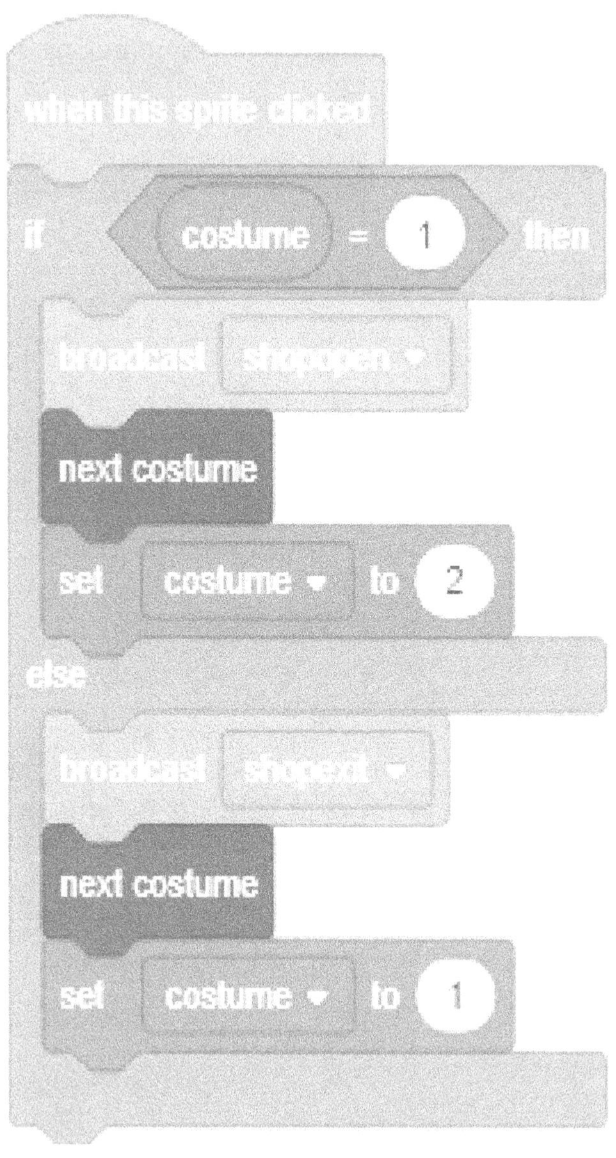
when this sprite clicked
if
costume
=
1
then
broadcast
shopopen
next costume
set
costume
to
2
else
broadcast
shopexit
next costume
set
costume
to
1

Now the shop button works.

Continuing Buildings Section

Create a cost variable, a sprite for the building, and a variable for the number of that building the user owns.

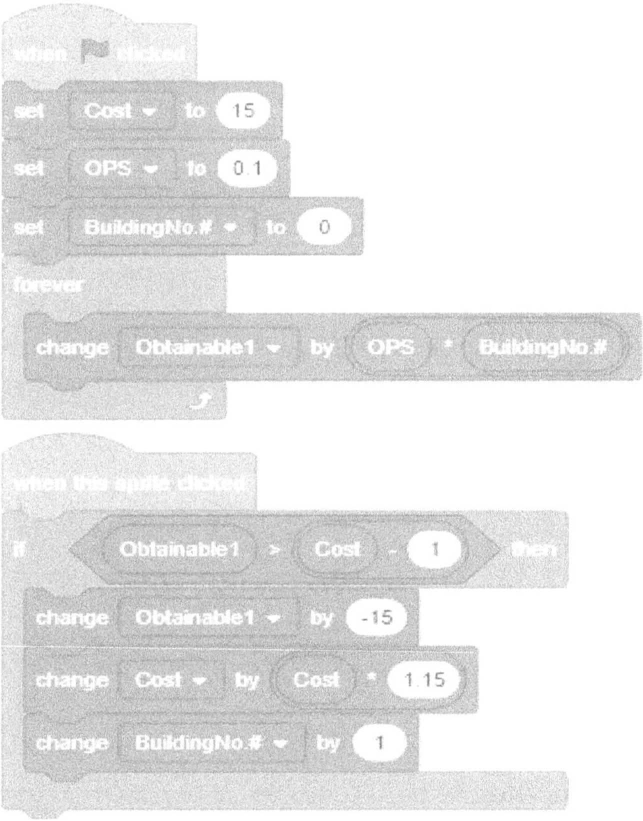

Button Section Continued

Add the following script to the buildings

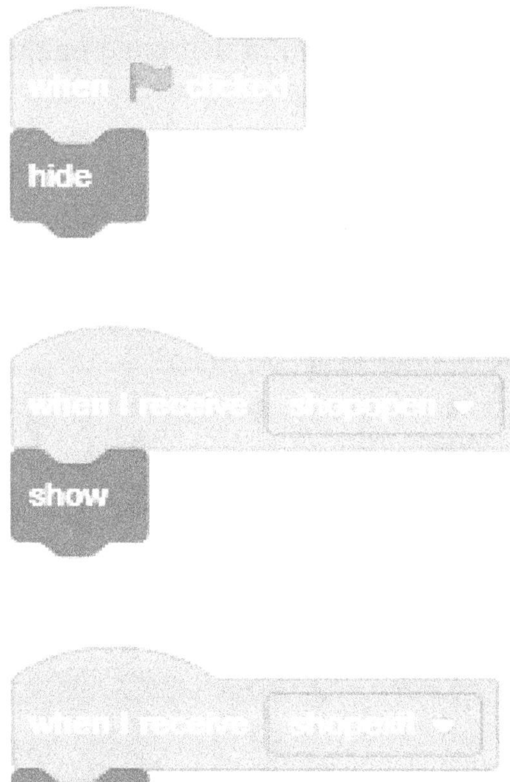

Achievements

Note: The following is optional to create.

Achievements are very hard to create a tutorial on, as they are triggered by different things. That is why this section is small. There is no proper tutorial of achievements for that reason..

Upgrades

Upgrades are hard to make. But, this section will walk you through upgrades.

It is easy to notice that this section is unfinished. That is because if a button is made, the Button section should also be seen.

Button Section

Add the following blocks as where they say to go.

Snap onto the when green flag clicked.

Snap onto the end.

Then, add the following script.

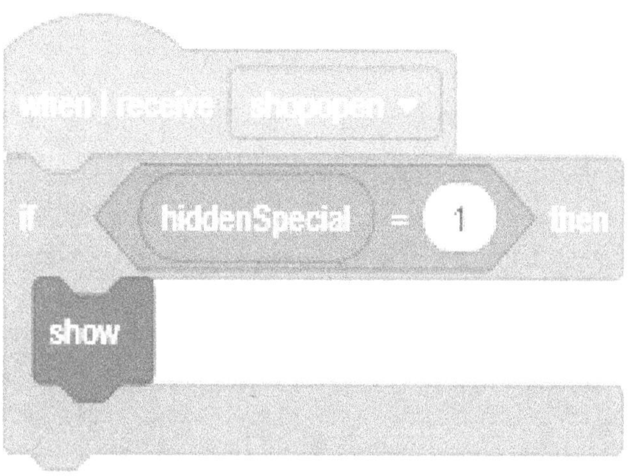

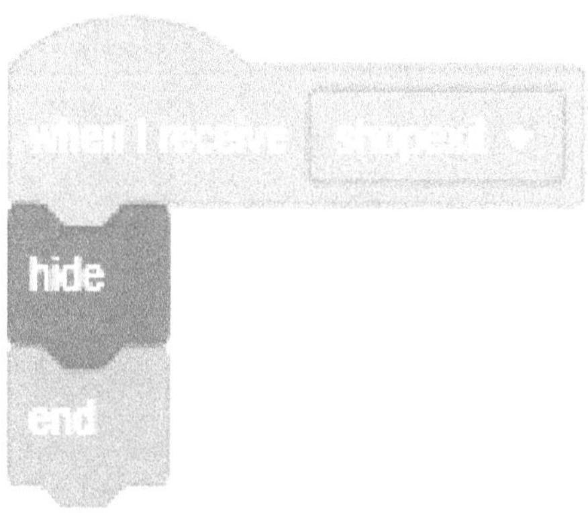

Upgrades Continued

Next, add the following script.

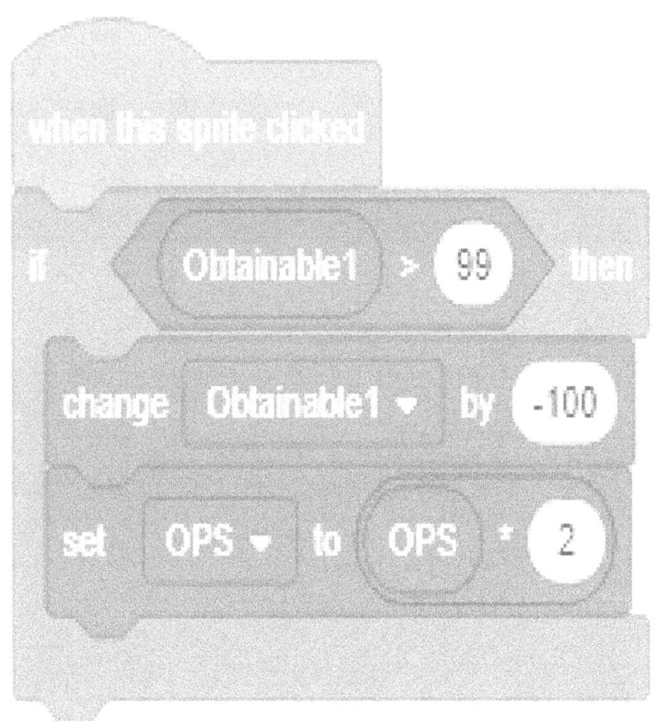

The "And Block

() and () block not only is an Operators block, but also Boolean block. If the blocks have to be true to return true, that means, the block joins two Boolean blocks. In case that the two are true, the block returns true. In the other hand, in case that they are not all true or none is true, it returns false.

The *() and () block* can pile up inside itself. You can use it not only for one condition but to test more conditions.

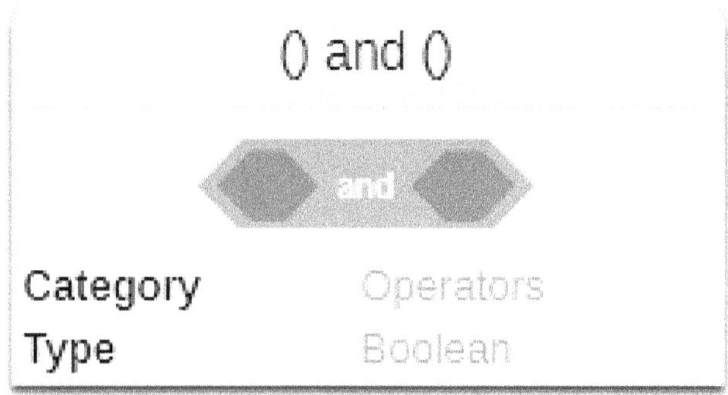

This block is used for checking if two or more conditions are true at the same time. Some cases of this are:

- No life if "In case that you touch the high voltage without a special glove."

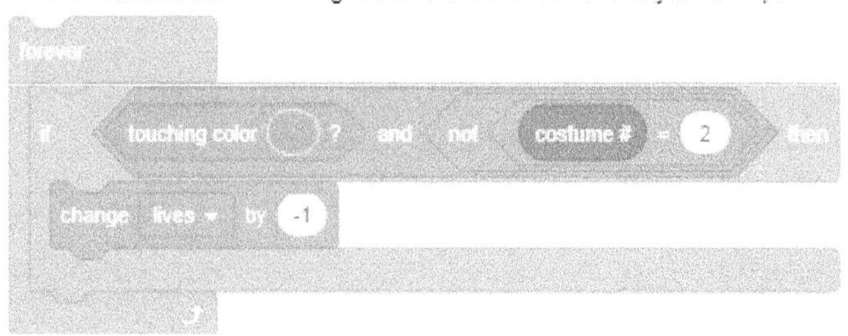

- When the mouse touches a button, it is clicked. And also the mouse is down.

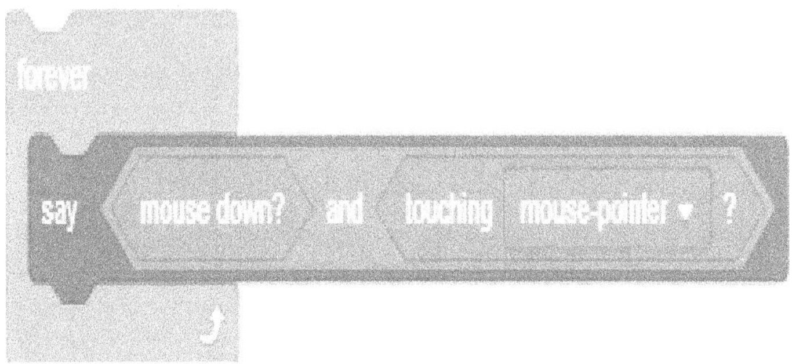

Workaround

This block can be totally replicated with the following code:

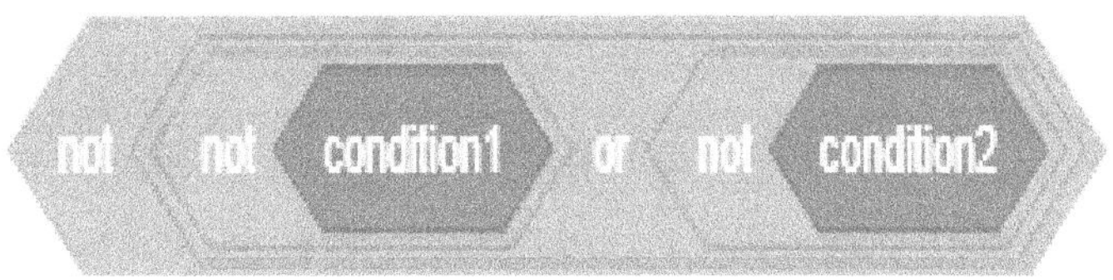

Another way to replicate this block is:

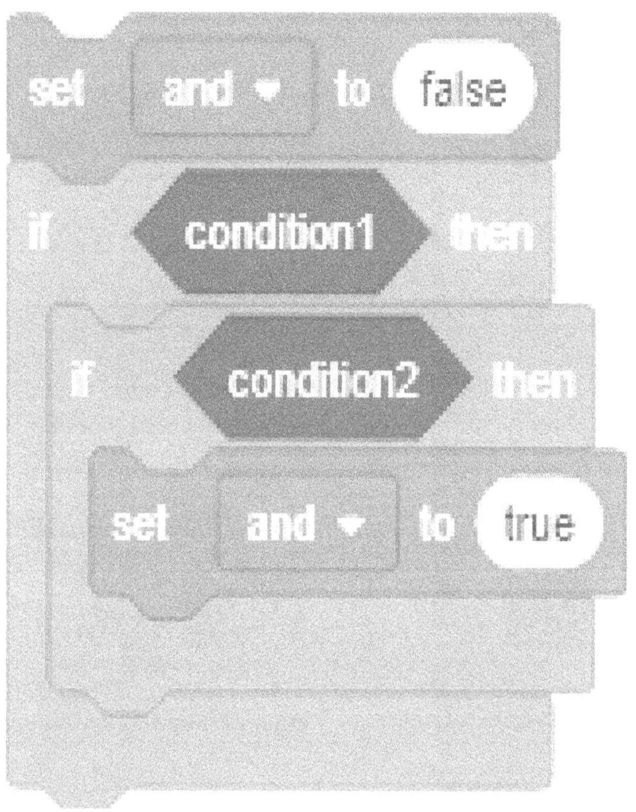
set
and
to
false
if
condition1
then
if
condition2
then
set
and
to
true

Project #3: Hedgehog Hedge Maze

Step #1: Using Scratch

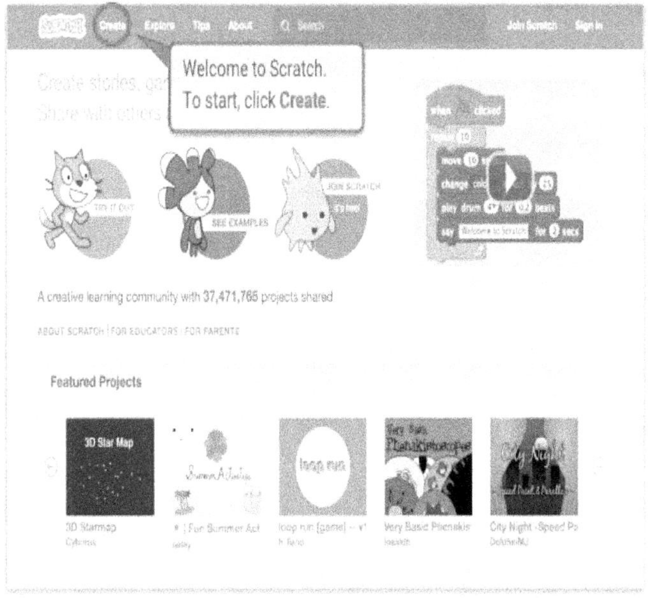

Step #1a: Creating your first project

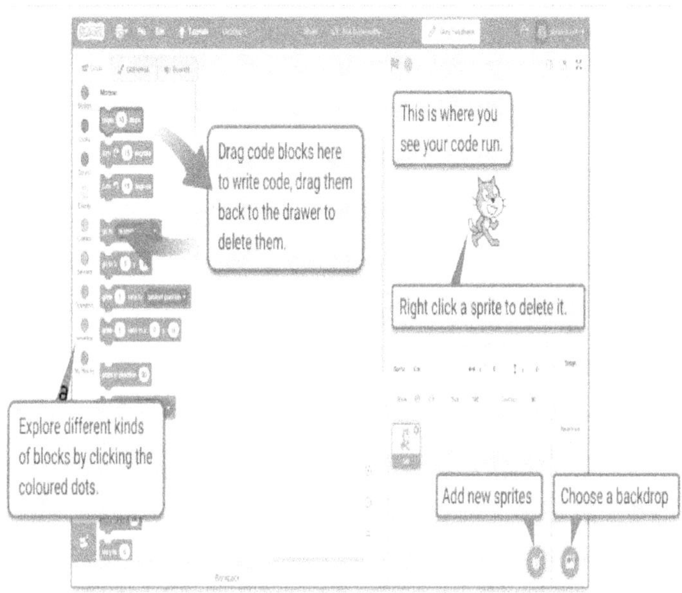

Step #1b: Working with sprites

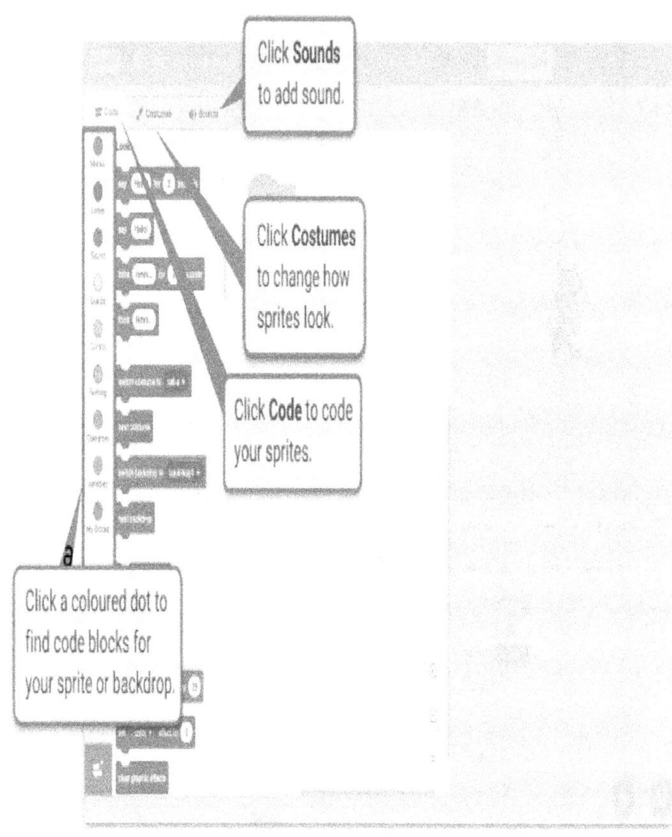

Step #1c: Adding some code

Drag out these blocks to see what will happen.

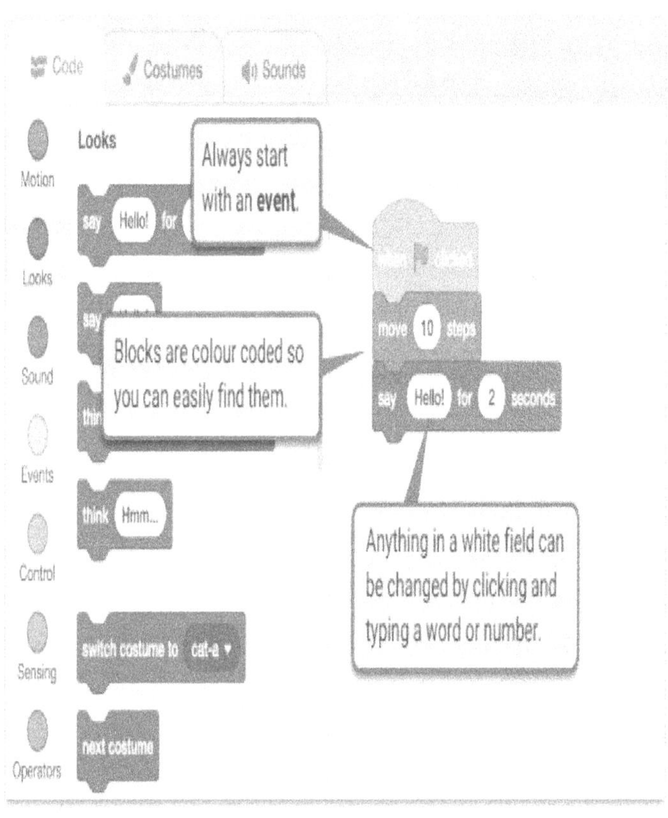

Step #1d: Designing sprites

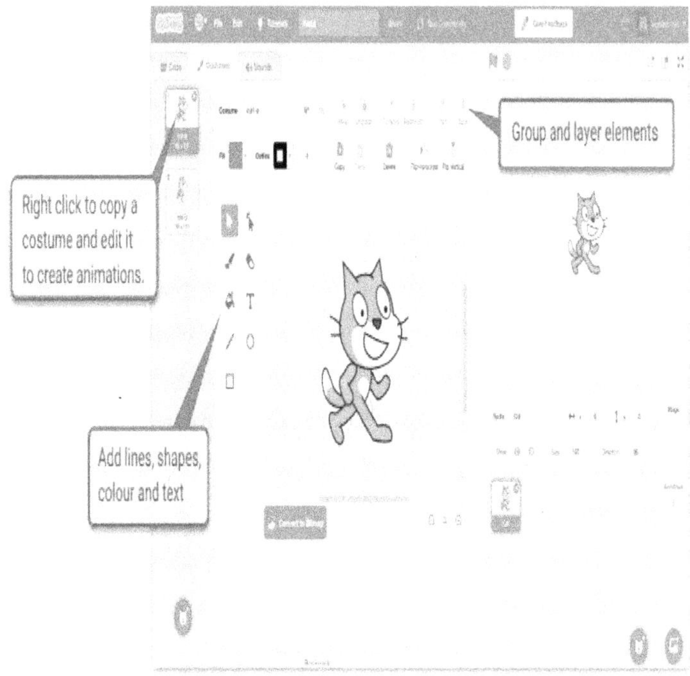

Step #2a: Code the arrow keys

- Select a new sprite
- Pull out the When space key pressed block from the events drawer
- Change the block so it says When right arrow key pressed

- Extract the change x by 10. You must do it from motion drawer.
- Click the blocks together.
- Test: press the right arrow key and see what happens.

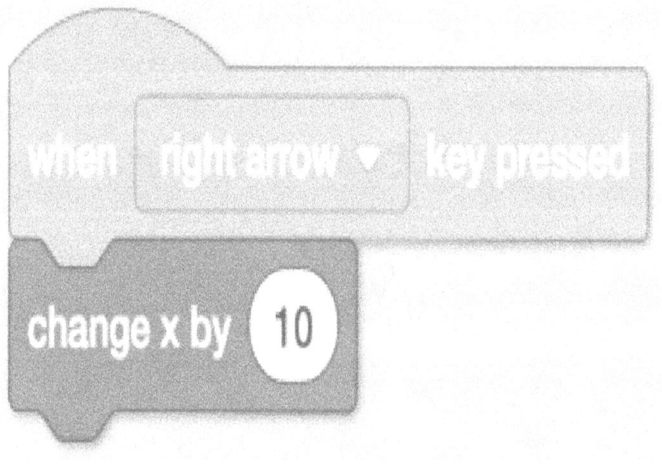

Step #2b: Code the arrow keys

- Press the space key block from the events drawer to drag a new
- From the motion drawer, you can bring a change y by 10 block

- Click them together
- Test: press the right arrow key and see what happens.

If you are ready, go ahead and code the down arrow and the left arrow (if you're not sure, you can see all the code on the next page).

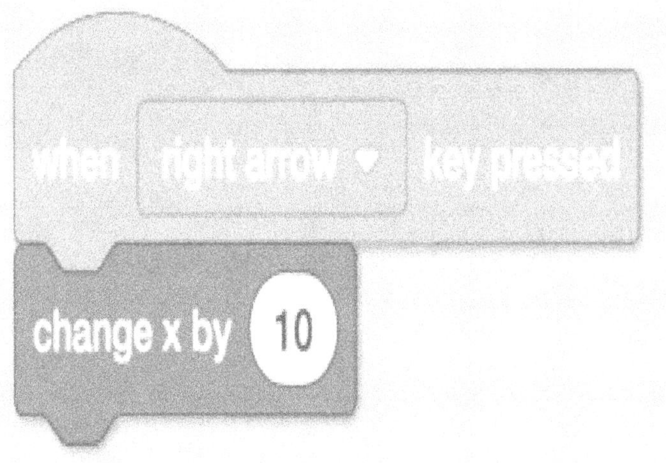

Checkpoint

Test: your sprite can move left, right, up and down using the arrow keys

Step #3: Draw the maze

Now it's time to draw a maze using the paint tools in Scratch.

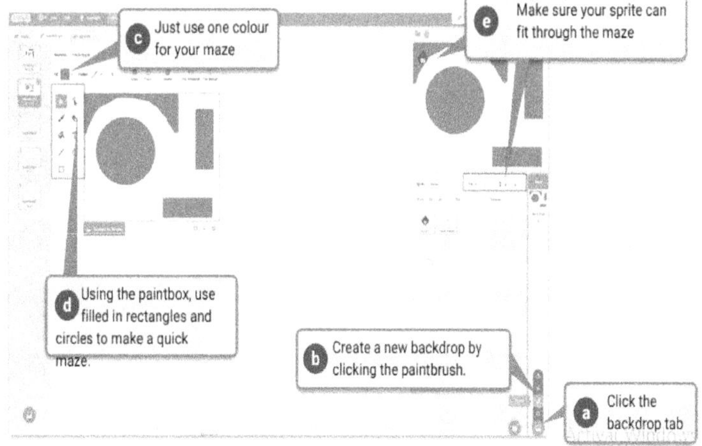

To check if your sprite touches the wall, choose an if...then block from the control drawer

- From the sensing drawer, bring out the touching colour block and add it to the if...then block as shown

- Click inside the coloured oval (purple here) then hovewover your maze so that the oval changes colour to be the same as the colour of your maze walls

- from the motion drawer, choose the go to x y block and add the numbers shown

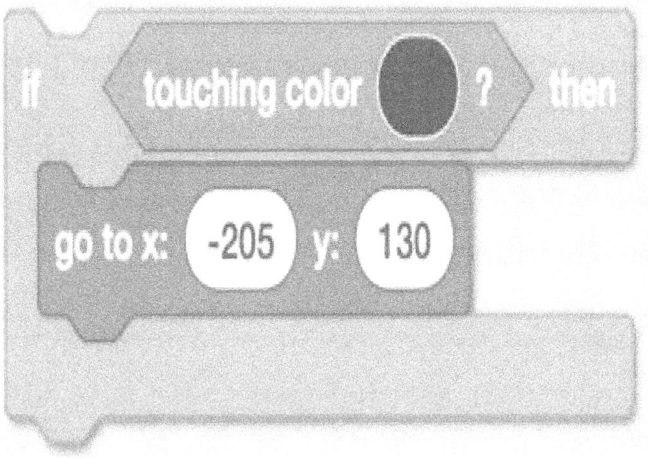

Step #4b: make the maze solid

To make sure the code checks all the time if the sprite is touching purple:

- Pull out a when green flag is clicked block from the event drawer.
- To start in the same place each time, pull out a go to x y block from the motion drawer
- Pull out a forever block from the control drawer
- Put the if...then code you already have inside the forever block

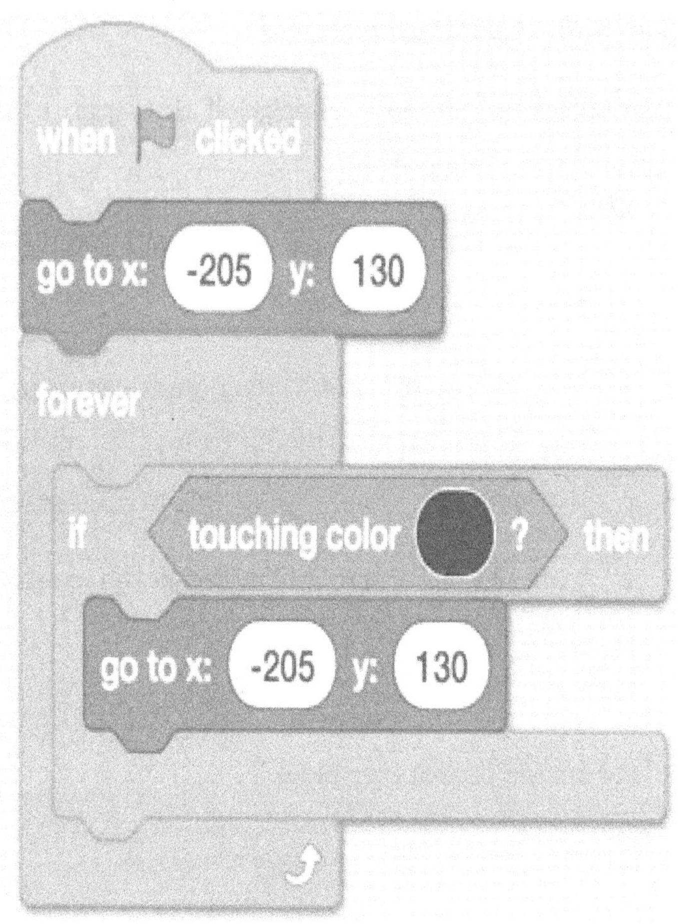

The final code is in Green Flag

Step #5: Add a beginning and end

- Test: guide your sprite through the maze. It should bounce off all, and when it reaches the end return to a go and deliver your message.
- To make an end point, the code is a bit like the code to make the walls solid.
- Draw a colored rectangle onto your backdrop - ours is pink
- Use an if...then block with a touching color block to check if the sprite has touched your end point
- Decide what happens: we used a go to x y block to return to the start,
- Add some words: find a say block in the looks drawer and add your own message
- You can also add a sound effect or change the way the sprite looks using

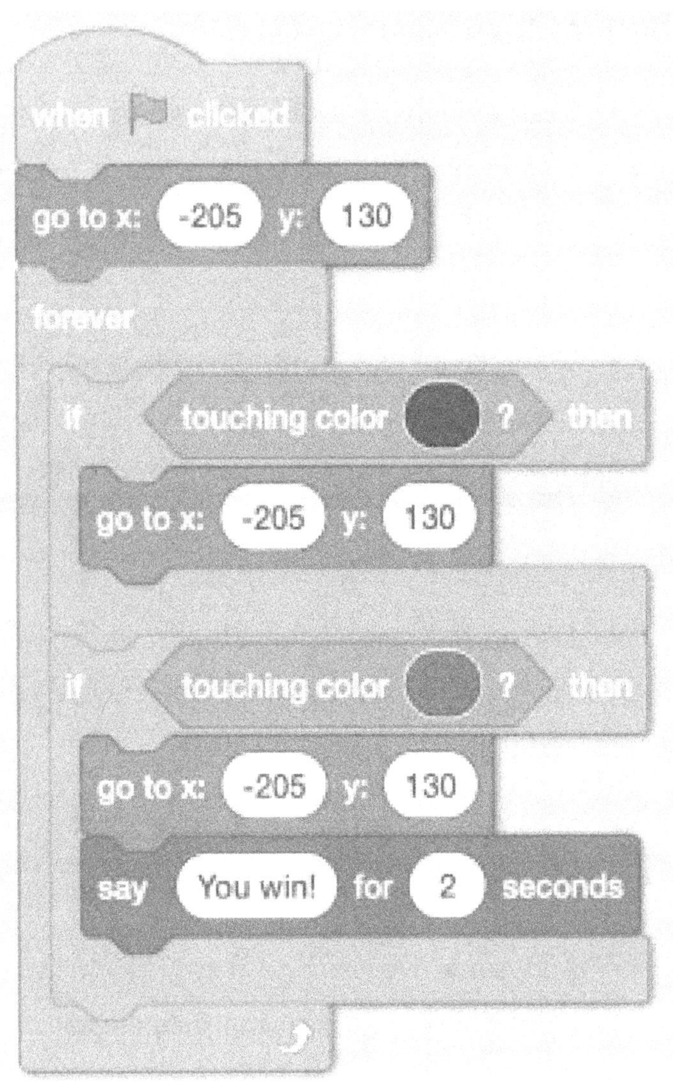

Step #6: Add variables

If you want your sprite to have lives, have a go adding this code to your project

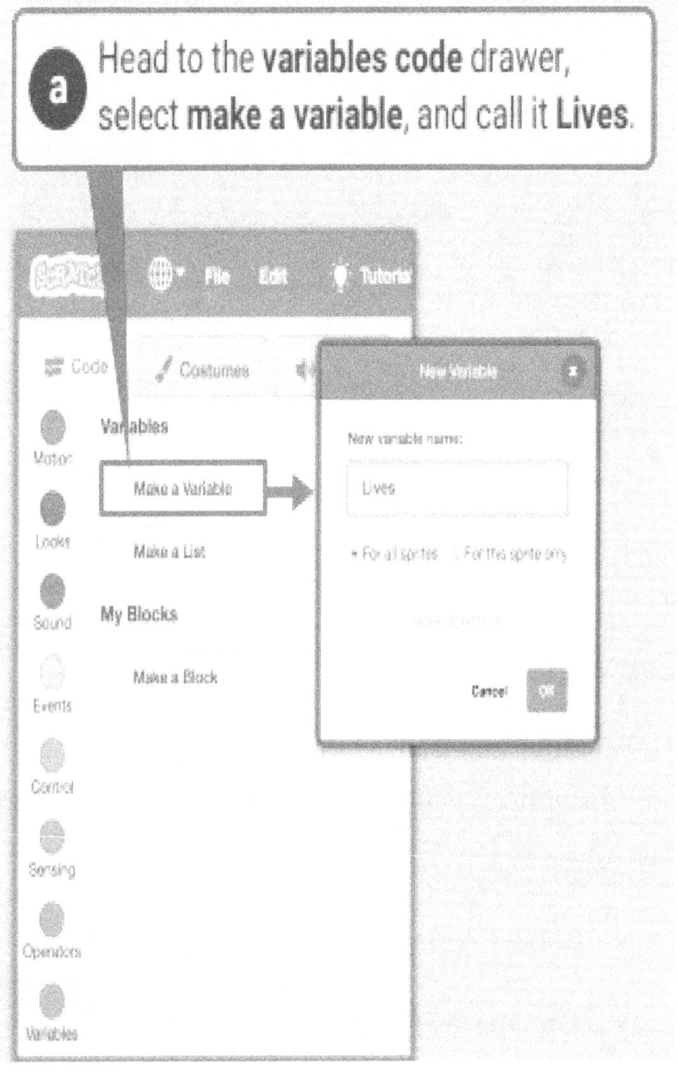

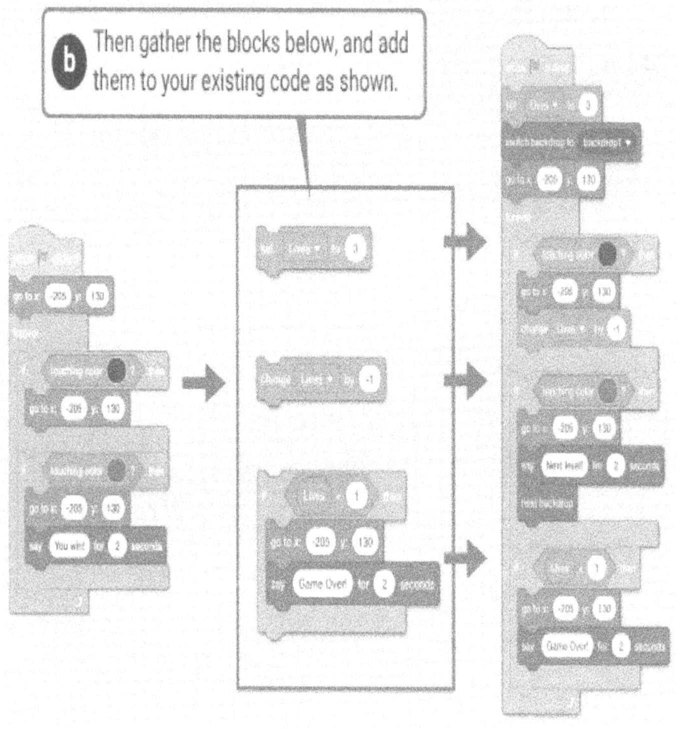

Step #7: Create tokens

How to add tokens to your maze? If you want to do so; for your sprite to collect, follow the steps below:

- Choose a new sprite
- The spaces to write its code exist for every sprite. You have to make sure you add code

in the right place. Another thing you must have clear, each character should have a blue rectangle around it

- Use a when green flag clicked block
- From the looks drawer pull out a hide block
- To extract a repeat block, go in the control drawer to do so.
- Also in control , find a create clone of myself block
- Put them together as shown

Step #8: Send tokens to random spots

This code tells each token where to go, and whether it should show or not.

- Pull out a when I start as a clone block from the events drawer
- Find a point in direction block and go to random position block in the motion drawer
- We use a different if block this time - if then else so that the token will hide if it's on the wall, or show if it's not
- Go to the control drawer to find the wait block
- The pick random 1 to 10 exist only in the operators drawer

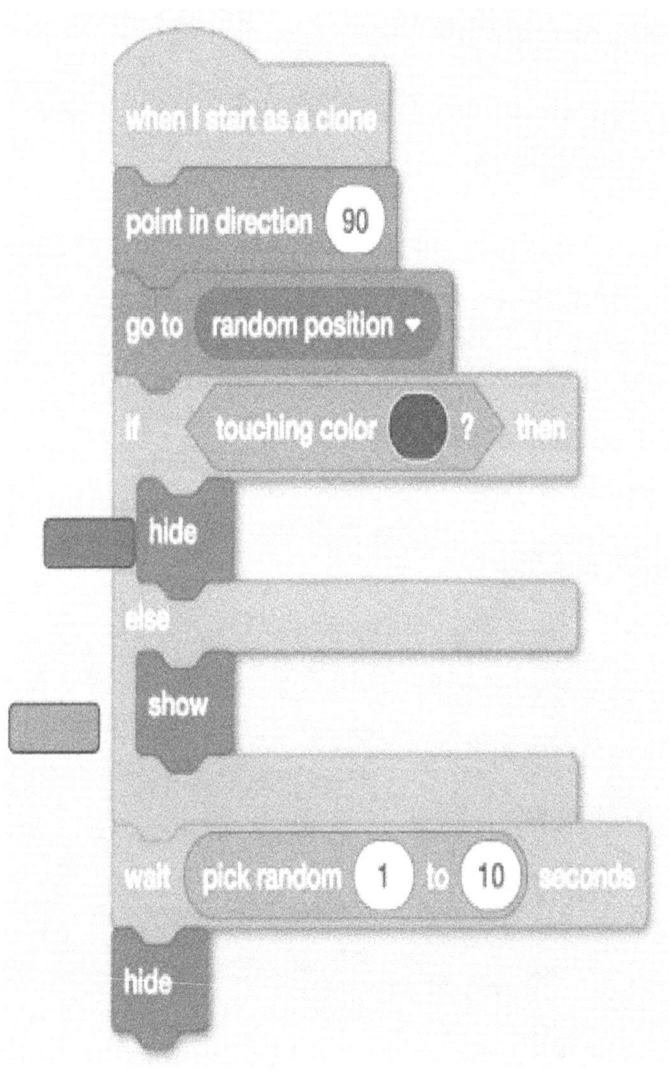
when I start as a clone
point in direction 90
go to random position
if touching color ? then
hide
else
show
wait pick random 1 to 10 seconds
hide

Step #9: Collect tokens

You can decide what happens when a sprite touches a token.

In our example the token spins around, changes size and colour, before hiding.

You can choose what happens to your token!

```
when I start as a clone
forever
  if <touching (Sprite1 ▾) ?> then
    repeat (30)
      turn ↻ (12) degrees
      change size by (-2)
      change [color ▾] effect by (5)
    end
    hide
  end
end
```

Chapter 4: Advanced Topics!

Broadcasts

In the events, it is where to find all the broadcast blocks. However, you will find them in Control palette in other version of Scratch, in Scratch 1.4 and earlier.

Broadcast ()

The previous block has no further effect and broadcasts the specified message.

Broadcast () and Wait

This block broadcasts the specified message and blocks its script until all scripts under

When I Receive ()

There will be no activity for this block until it receives the specified broadcast. For the script to go in action and ends it when it has finish, it has to receive the specified broadcast. However, it can start more than once.

() Received?

The non-existent Boolean block is "() Received? (Or I Receive ()) block". Many Scratchers have requested it. This block would most likely belong in the Sensing category, or possibly the Control category. However, the Scratch Team has rejected it too ambiguous.

Three possible appearances of the () Received? block

It is also possible to make a substitute for this block as seen below:

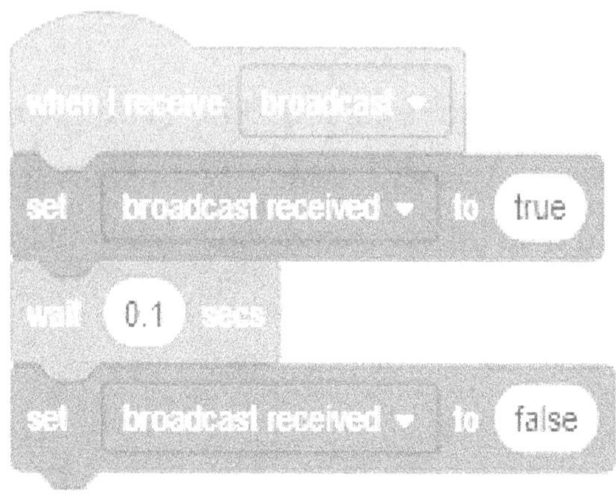

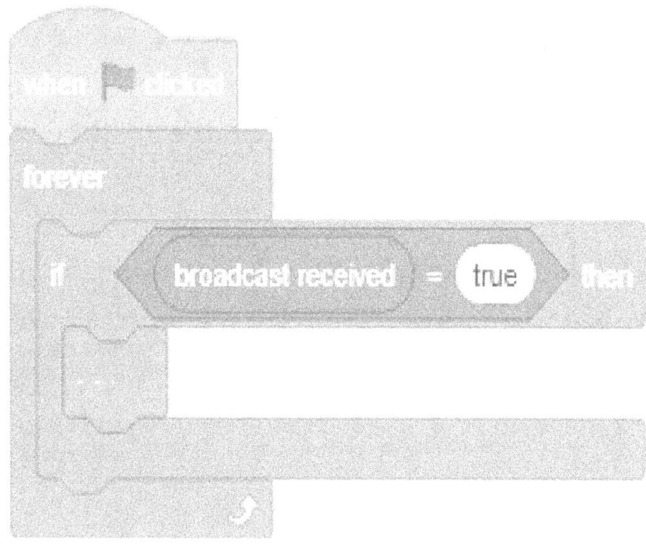

For the code to work, you must use a variable *broadcast_received* to keep track of when a broadcast is received. In case that a broadcast is received, the variable is ready to "true" for long enough that each one scripts can run a minimum of once. All scripts will check broadcast_received and see that a broadcast was received.

Broadcasting to Specific Sprites

It is impossible for Scratch to limit where a broadcast can go. The global variable contains who receives the broadcast. It also has a private variable for each sprite and the id of that sprite. So, you can solve the above mentioned with that global variable. In case that, not only the ID but also the receiver match for a specific sprite, the broadcast is carried out. In the other hand, the broadcast is ignored by the sprite.

when clicked
broadcast init
On the Stage

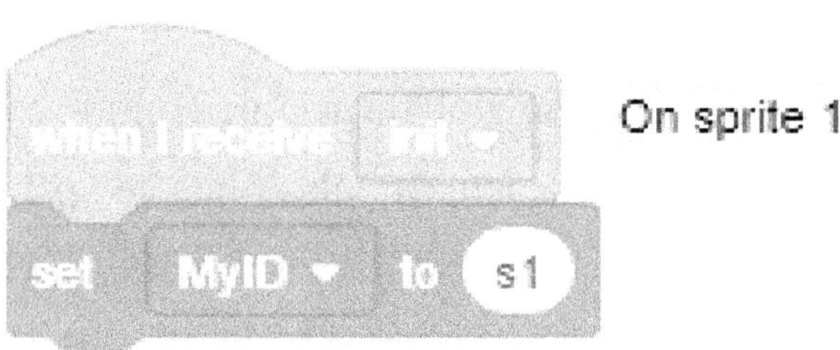
when I receive init
set MyID to s1
On sprite 1

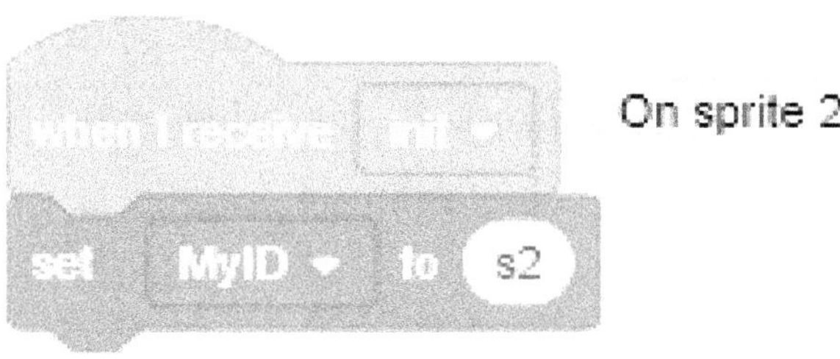
when I receive init
set MyID to s2
On sprite 2

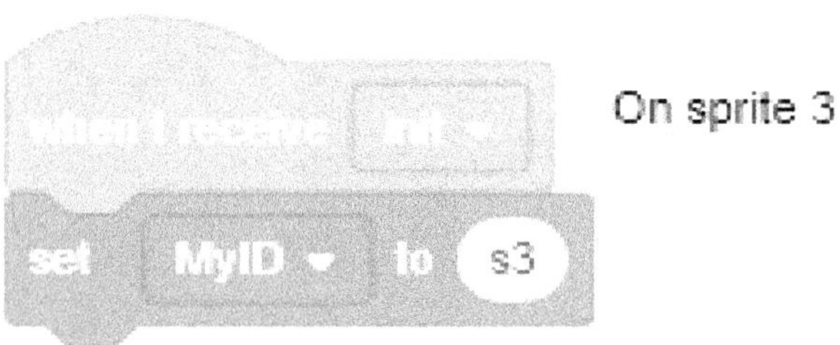
when I receive init
set MyID to s3
On sprite 3

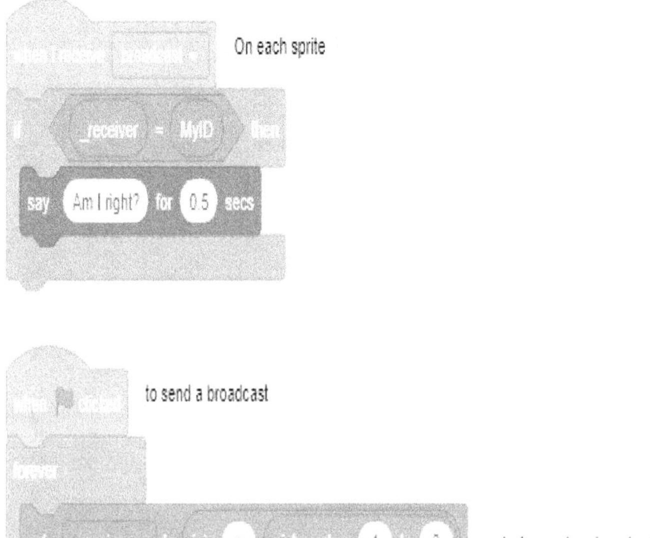

It is possible to automatically set the MyID variables rather than change the value for each sprite. This is useful when there are many identical sprites, for example, if there are many bubbles floating on the screen. Let's create a global variable such "IDconstr" to switch the "init" broadcast handler.

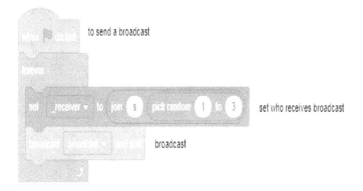

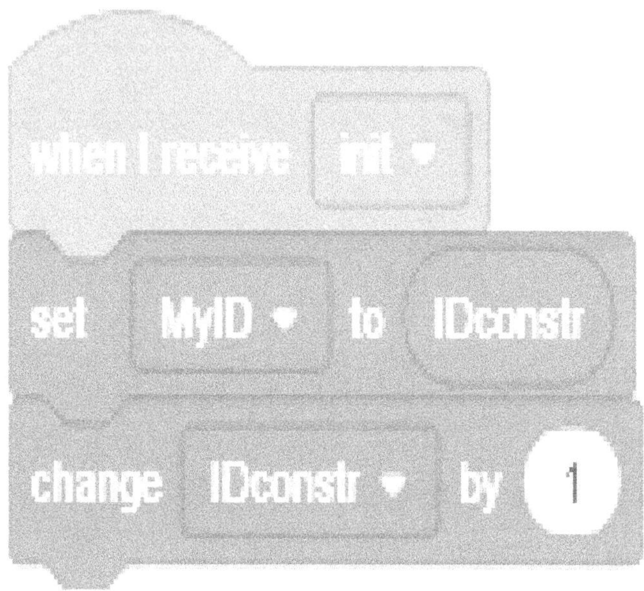

The If-Then-Else Block

These blocks will send the program in one way or another, depending on whether a condition is met, as in BASIC, there are two types of conditionals, some simpler if ... then and some more complex if ... then ... else.

In Scratch 1.4, this block was named If (), Else.

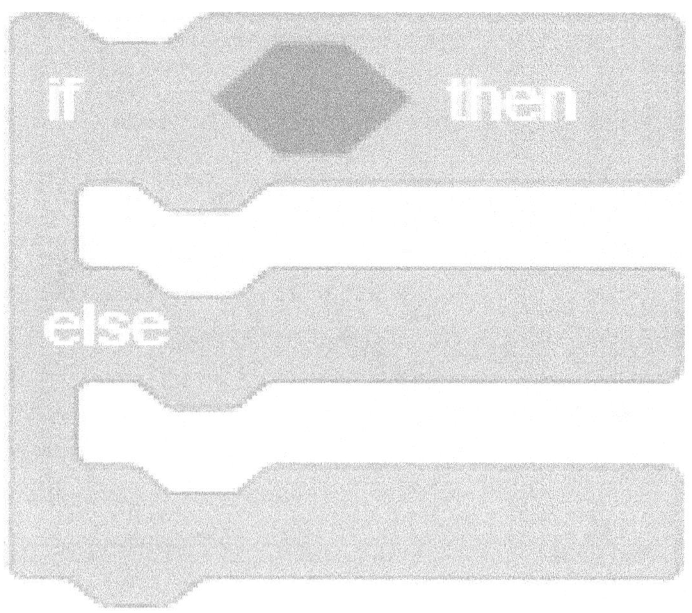

In programming, a very important part is "checking conditions." this is done with the If () block. However, an important part of the "checking conditions" is having another piece of code that runs if the condition is false. While this may be worked around, the If (), Else block makes this simpler. Some common uses:

Do "this" (the code inside the first C) or "that" (the code inside the second C)

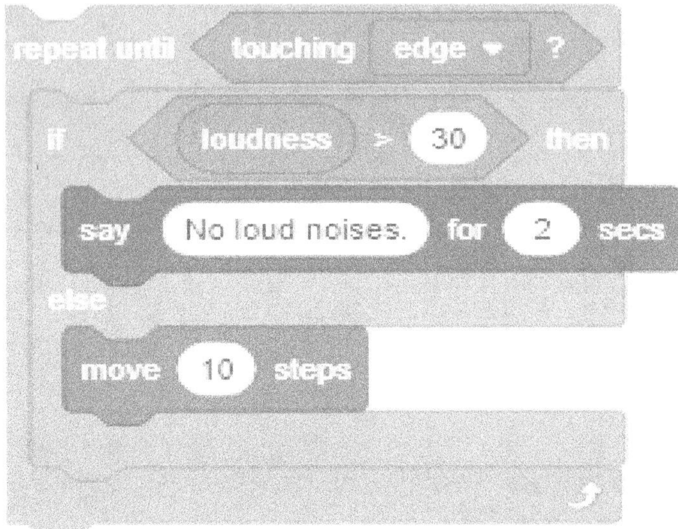

If a Sprite's health is below a certain amount, it dies, otherwise it does something else

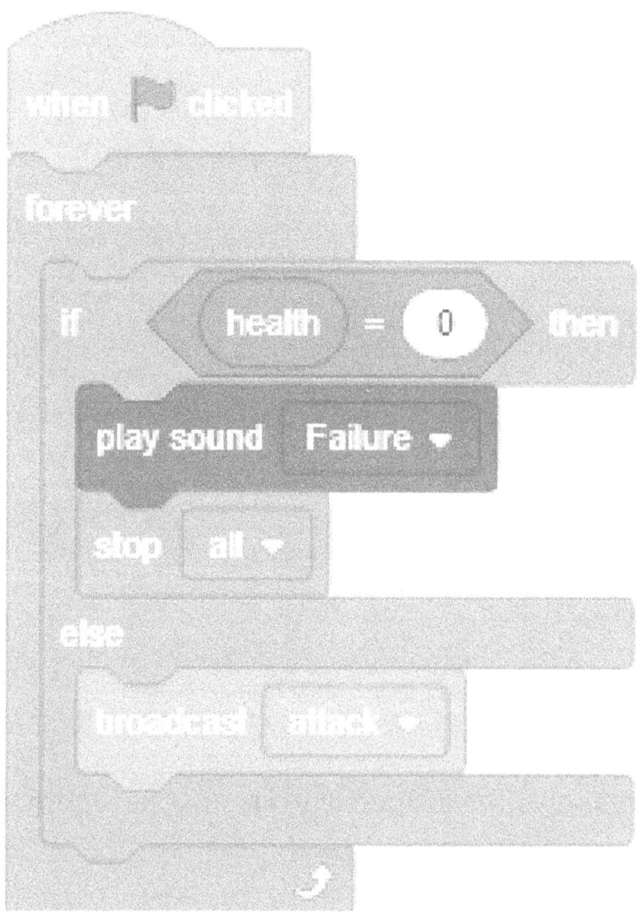

Easy script changes — if a variable equals a certain value, one thing happens, and if the variable does not equal the value, a different thing happens

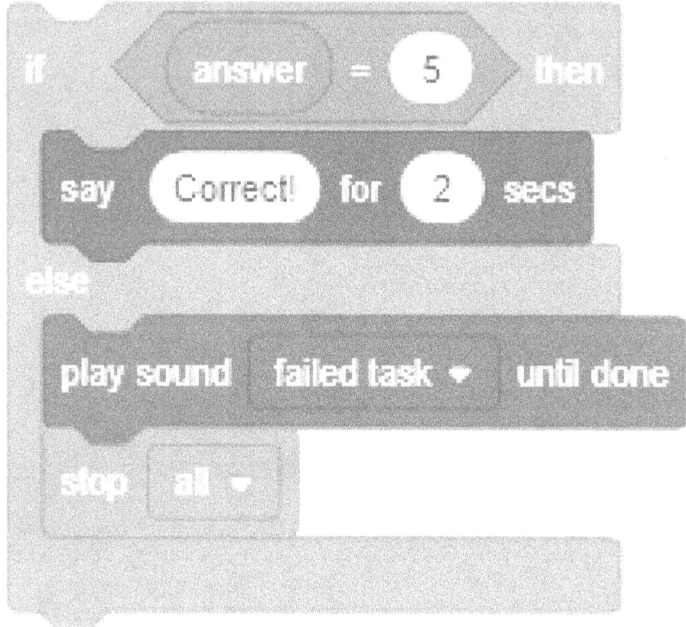

Scripts that are adaptable to changes in conditions (such as a changing variable)

if
touching color
?
then
say
We found water!
else
say

() or () (block)

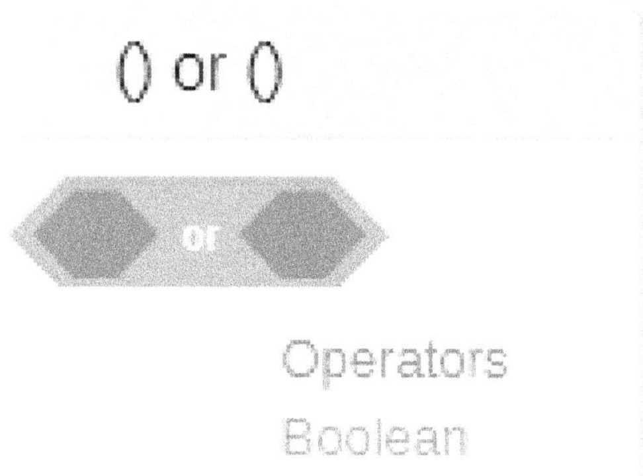

This script asks the user what their favorite color, and will give one response if it is "blue" or "red", and another response if it is anything else.

```
when [flag] clicked
ask What is your favorite color? and wait
if answer = blue or answer = red then
  say I also like that color!
else
  say That's a nice color!
```

Workaround

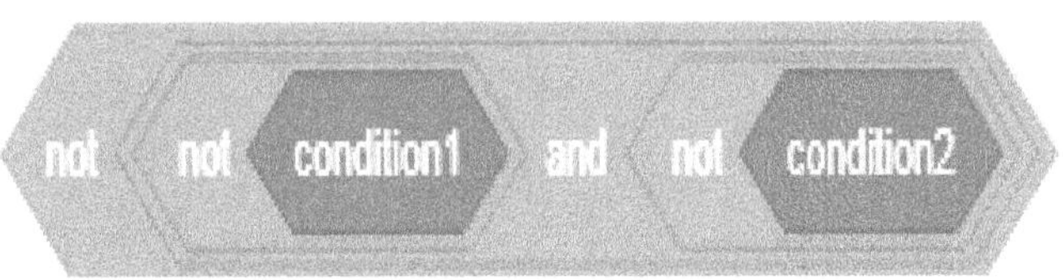

This stack also works (with the variable T/F being the result):

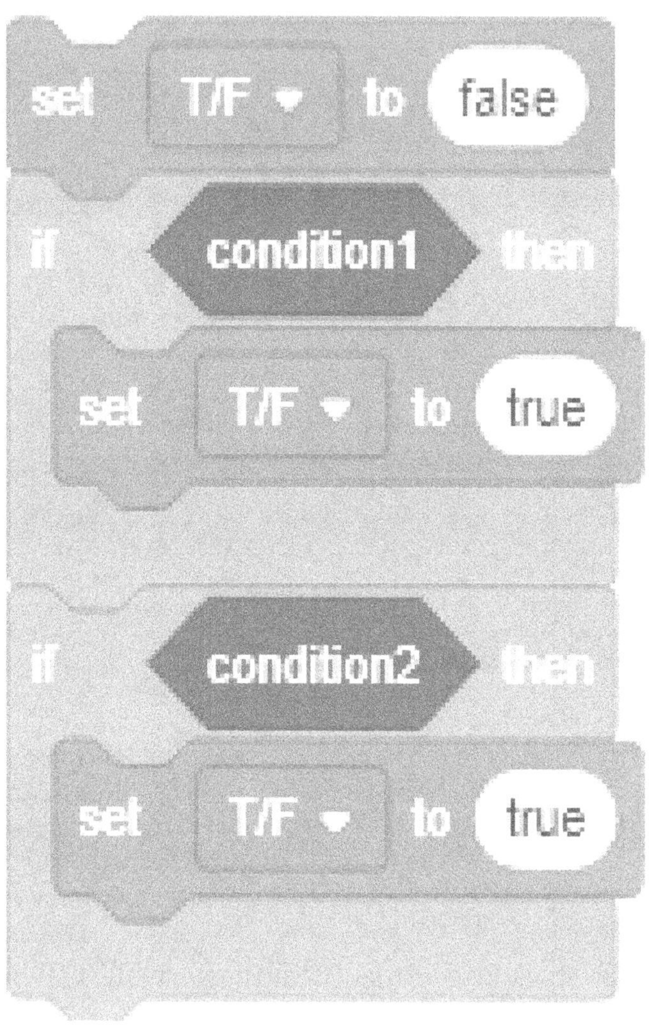
set T/F to false
if condition1 then
set T/F to true
if condition2 then
set T/F to true

Chapter 5: Artificial Intelligence: Machine Learning

Machine learning tool for kids to develop artificial intelligence systems and incorporate them into digital creations with Scratch 3.0.

Technology

The tool is based entirely on the web and requires neither installation nor complex configuration to use.

It was designed for use in the classroom, both in schools and in children's programming clubs run by volunteers, and provides an administration page for teachers or group leaders to manage and manage their students' access.

Development is carried out by Dale Lane using IBM Watson Developer Cloud APIs.

What do offer this tool?

This tool offers an introduction to machine learning through practical experiences to train machine learning systems and build things with them.

It consists of a simple guided learning environment to train machine learning models capable of identifying text, numbers or images.

It complements the existing efforts to introduce and teach children to program, adding these models to Scratch (the educational programming platform used worldwide), allowing children to create projects and build games with the machine learning models that they have trained themselves.

Why?

Machine learning is everywhere. People use it daily in their life. For example, spam detection filters, recommendation systems, language translation services, chatbots and digital assistants, search engines, and fraud detection systems.

It will soon be normal for machine learning systems to drive our cars and help doctors diagnose and treat our diseases.

Children must know how the world works. The best way to understand the capabilities and implications of machine learning is to use this technology to build something.

Scratch-based Artificial Intelligence/ Machine Learning

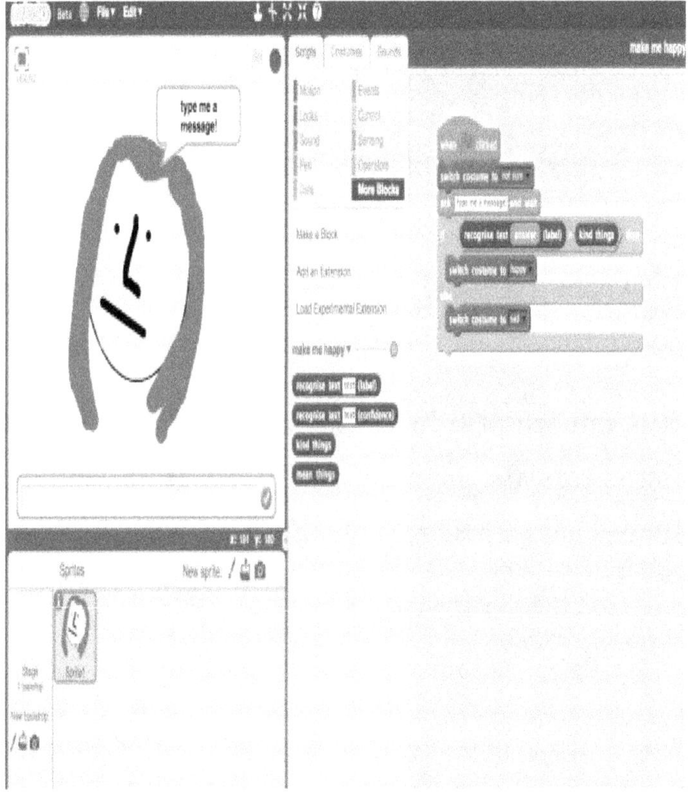

The AlphaGo system

The AlphaGo system is a remarkable feat of computer science. However, it is a common misconception that all machine learning algorithms are like this.

Every program starts with this block, all it means that when I click start, the program will run:

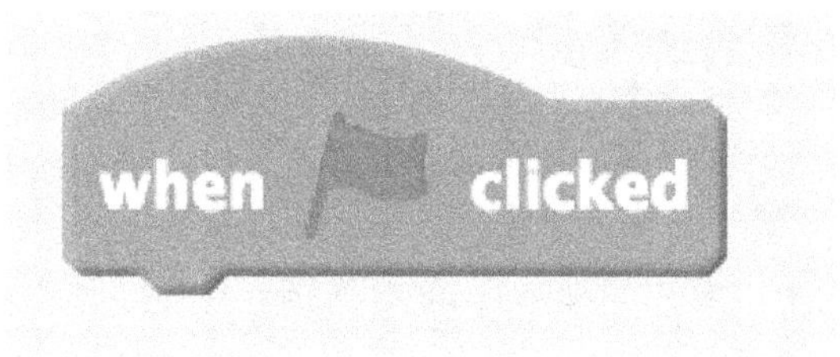

Use some of twelve blocks with a little casual conversation

It is important to note the second block however, this clears the memory of the program, so each time is uses a new set of y-values:

```
when [flag] clicked
delete all of y-values
say Hello! for 2 secs
say I am a Machine Learning algorithm that picks up correlations between two sets of data for 5 secs
say I will tell you x-values, and I want you to put in the corresponding y-values for 2 secs
```

simply ask for the y-value for when x equals one or two, and they are added to my list of y-values:

```
when [flag] clicked
delete all of y-values
say Hello! for 2 secs
say I am a Machine Learning algorithm that picks up correlations between two sets of data for 5 secs
say I will tell you x-values, and I want you to put in the corresponding y-values for 2 secs
ask 1 and wait
add answer to y-values
ask 2 and wait
add answer to y-values
```

The important part is the following! The program uses the values it has just collected to work out the gradient and y-intercept of the graph, using the regression technique we looked at earlier.

Please note that, because the x-values are predetermined, their difference will be 1. Therefore, when calculated the gradient, it is not divided by the change in x like you normally would.

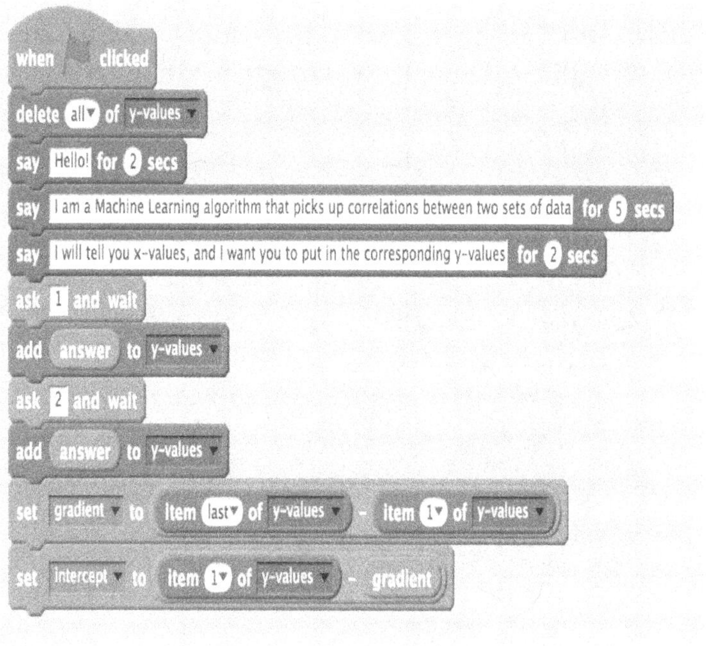

```
when [flag] clicked
delete (all) of [y-values]
say [Hello!] for (2) secs
say [I am a Machine Learning algorithm that picks up correlations between two sets of data] for (5) secs
say [I will tell you x-values, and I want you to put in the corresponding y-values] for (2) secs
ask [1] and wait
add (answer) to [y-values]
ask [2] and wait
add (answer) to [y-values]
set [gradient] to ((item (last) of [y-values]) - (item (1) of [y-values]))
set [intercept] to ((item (1) of [y-values]) - (gradient))
```

Finally, plug the variables when we have calculated the equation y = mx + c, to get my result for when x = 3:

```
when [flag] clicked
delete (all) of [y-values]
say [Hello!] for (2) secs
say [I am a Machine Learning algorithm that picks up correlations between two sets of data] for (5) secs
say [I will tell you x-values, and I want you to put in the corresponding y-values] for (2) secs
ask [1] and wait
add (answer) to [y-values]
ask [2] and wait
add (answer) to [y-values]
set [gradient] to ((item (last) of [y-values]) - (item (1) of [y-values]))
set [intercept] to ((item (1) of [y-values]) - (gradient))
say [I have calculated that when x= 3, y would equal] for (4) secs
say (((gradient) * (3)) + (intercept))
```

There we have it! In just a few lines of the simplest programming language in the world we have built an AI!

The Extra Code

Now, I know this is technically over the quota from the title, but I couldn't resist. This extra piece of code allows you to put in your own values:

```
when space key pressed
ask Please input a value: and wait
say gradient * answer + intercept
```

It works in exactly the same way as the main code, it just uses a user input value instead of the preassigned 3.

Chapter 6: Make Your Game Fun!

Creating a Basic Mario Game with scratch

Instructions:

Control the witch's movement with the right, left, up and down arrow keys to dodge dragons and capture as many stars as possible.)

To start, if you do not have a user on the Scratch website you should create one, so that you can save your games and creations to edit them in the future, share them with the community, receive comments and ratings, etc. Once you have logged in, you will click on the Create section of the web to start a new project.

The simple Mario Game example below shows how you can use blocks to control sprites. For this reason, we can learn more about it when creating a simple Mario game. We could spend thousands of words on every aspect of making a game, so we'll stick to the basics.

Please note: if you are not an artist, for the purposes of this game you can copy Mario sprites from the web. It is forbidden to publish any game that copyrighted sprites with Mario graphics. This is presented as an example only.

Import Graphics

Import y or sprites and backgrounds in scratch is the first step you must five. Since we're using images from the web, we will download them and then upload them into Scratch. In this game, we'll have him collect coins instead of creating logical so that Mario can jump on enemies to defeat them.

Here are the sprites that we downloaded:

- Mario running (two frames is sufficient for us)
- Mario jumping
- Animated coin
- Ground blocks
- Clouds

There are also that will work for us and that will be our needs. There are the Blue Sky 3 backgrounds.

Edit Sprite Costumes

Because there are two sprites that make up Mario's run animation, you need to add them as separate costumes. Use an image editor like Paint.NET to save the two Mario frames as separate files — you can ignore the third. Choose the first Mario sprite and upload it. Do the same for the second sprite choosing it in Costumes tab as the second costumes. Give them distinguishable names, like Mario-1 and Mario-2. Now, the jumping sprite as another costume for Mario can be put.

From the image provided above, you can use an image editor to extract the cloud. After doing so, you can upload it as a new sprite. As it's not animated; it is not necessary to add a separate costume.

Remember that, Mario will run on the ground. For this, it necessary to have lot of blocks because he will run along them. Use Paint.NET to grab the six blocks in the middle of the Ground Blocks image, then save them as a separate file. Let's say you have to use approximately about 12 blocks. The idea is to cover the complete bottom of the screen once you shrink them to a good size. Divide the blocks making stack of 6 and place two side-by-sides for your Ground sprite. Make two ground sprites duplicating in Scratch Upload the previous step mentioned.

The coin is an animated GIF, so it's a little different. Scratch will create costumes for every frame of the animation when you upload it. This image has 11 total frames, but Even if you see that this image has a white border around it, which looks off against the blue background, it has in total 11 frames. What does that means? We will need to get access to each costume for the coin inside the Scratch editor. Use the pipette tool to select the blue background color, then use the paint bucket tool to change the white edges of the coin to pale blue.

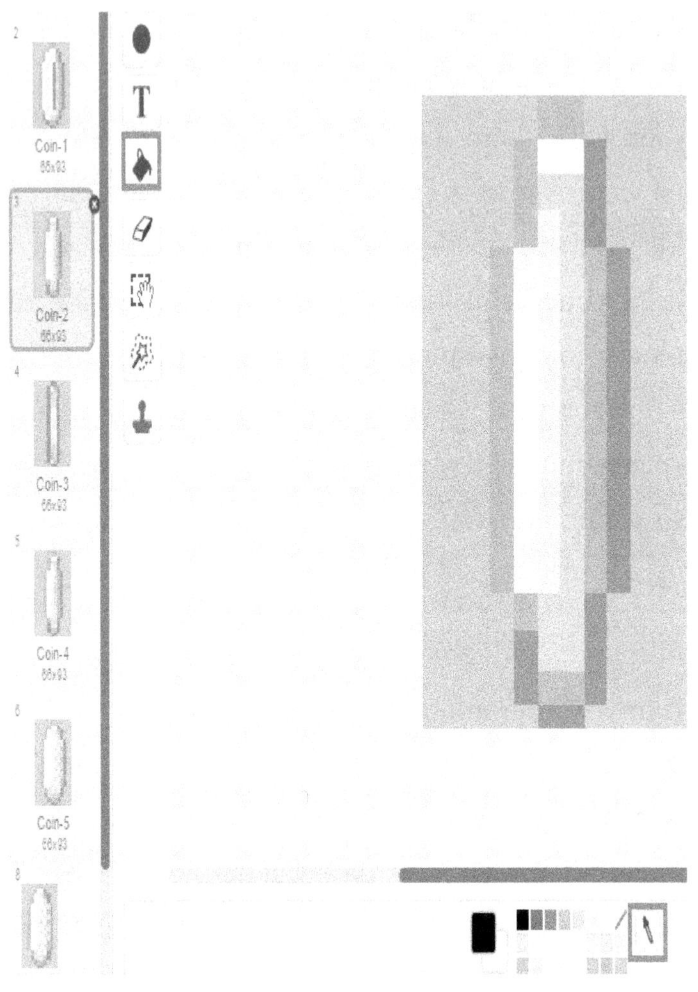

Along the top of the screen, there are the Grow and Shrink buttons. With them, you must resize the sprites. Those buttons are above the green flag button. Click either button, and then click the sprite you want to change on the stage to the left. This will resize all costumes, too. Ballpark them for now; you can fine-tune later.

Import Sounds

To flesh your game, you must grab sounds. You can import the sound to do so. But to upload them, use the Sounds tab.

- Super Mario Bros. Theme
- Mario jump sound
- Coin collect sound
- Animate the Coins

Now that all of the assets are ready, it's time to start making them come alive. It's better to start with the most difficult such as the coins. The others are easier. Select the coin sprite and the Scripts tab. Since our coins are animated GIFs, we can use a series of blocks to constantly scroll through their costumes so they appear to move.

An animation script looks something like this:

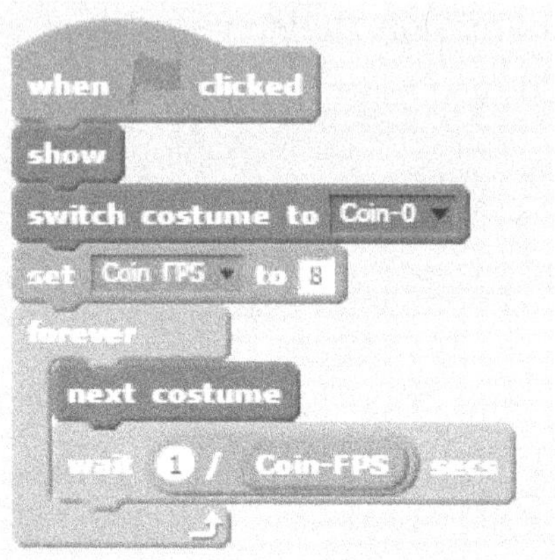

Click the green flag so that the above script can set the coin to its default state. It then cycles through the frames endlessly, at a speed you set as the FPS variable in the Data tab. Play around with that number if you don't like the speed.

Look the Data tab, and uncheck the box next to Coin-FPS. The reason why you don't see it in the screen it because it is a custom variable you create.

Making Mario Move

Now we're getting the hard part. Many steps are involved in making Mario move, and it's actually a trick that scrolls the ground blocks to give the appearance of movement. Rather than try to explain every block loop, we will provide screenshots of code blocks and explain their highlights.

First, you need to make four variables in the Data tab. Must know that, those four variables are for all sprites except for Velocity, which is only for Mario:

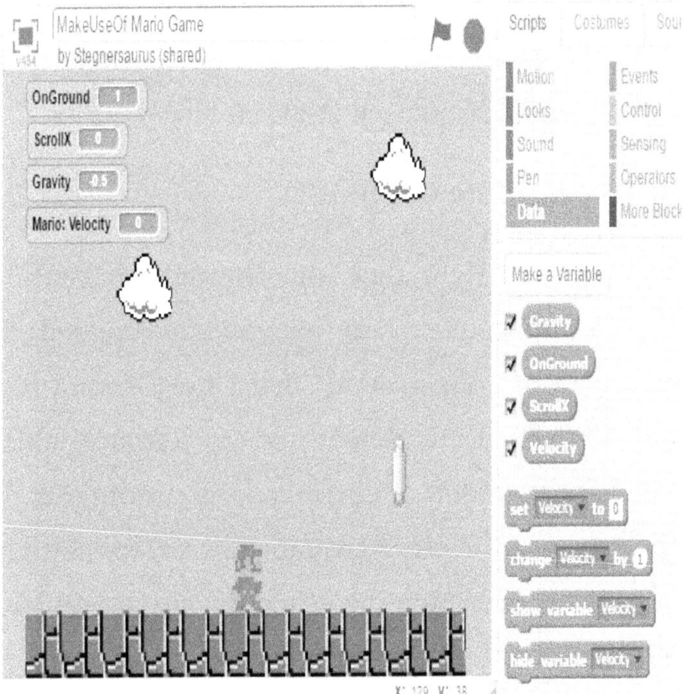

- ***Gravity:*** is a constant that pulls Mario back to the ground when he jumps.
- ***OnGround:*** *Thisv variables if to* kcep tracking of whether Mario is touching the ground or not.
- ***ScrollX:*** This variable is used to measure the horizontal movement of the screen.
- ***Velocity:*** This variable is for Mario only. It controls the speed at which Mario jumps.

Animating the Ground

Making the right-click on Ground sprite and choose duplicate explain that you have created the duplicate of your ground. Bring the Ground-1 to the far left of the screen, so its leftmost block touches the far left of the screen. After doing so, do the same for the other ground sprite(s) to the right of the first one. Line the edges up, and it will look like the ground is one solid piece.

Here's the code block you'll need for each Ground sprite:

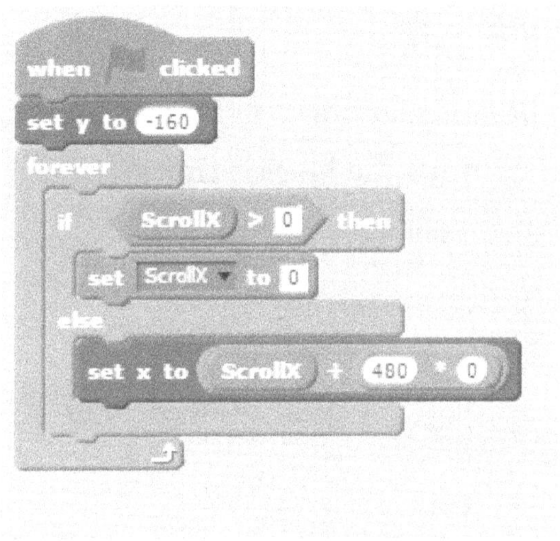

As Mario move, all you need to do is to scroll the blocks. The code above places the ground at the bottom of the screen. Don't forget that we have seen previously the utility of ScrollX. But in this case, it is represent the position of the blocks. 0 is the default position that launches when you click the green flag. You'll notice that you can't move left immediately after you start.

For the second (and further) ground blocks, increment the 0 digit in ScrollX + 480 * 0 by one for each new piece of ground. This will offset it so it scrolls smoothly.

Mario's Logic

Well, Mario has many more code blocks, but now, that's all we need for the blocks. However, here's what each of them do, with a brief summary:

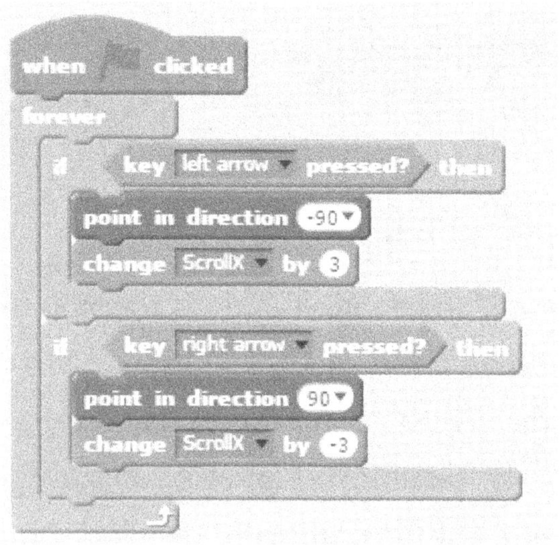

When Mario moves, the ScrollX variable can be changed by this block of code. Mario Take a step, incrementing **Scroll X by 3**. Also Mario faces in the appropriate direction. This is possible when you press left or right. Click the blue i on his sprite.

Also, make sure the Rotation still is set to the second option in case that you see Mario is upside down when you move left. Instead of a circle this will turn left and right.

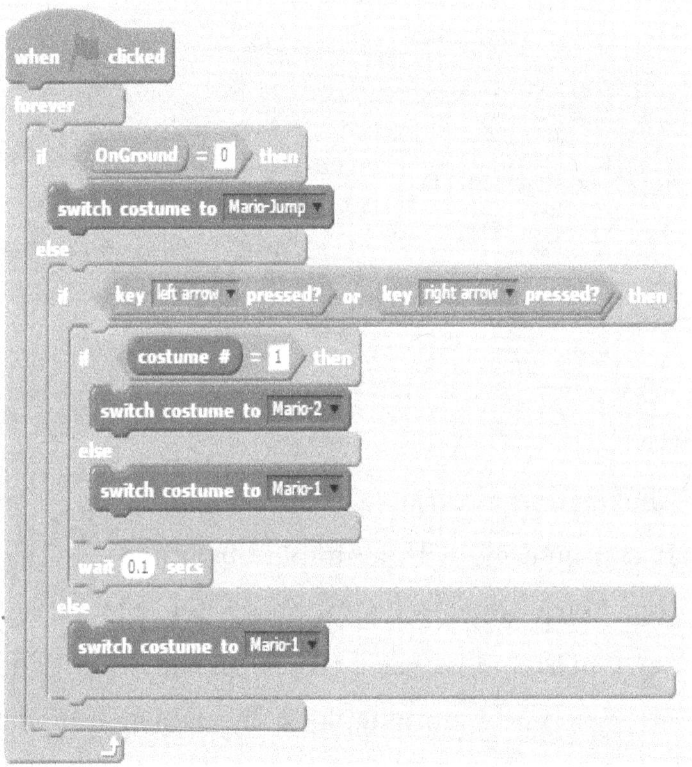

Mario's costume changes are visible by us thanks to the code that handles him. Mario jumps costume when he is not on the ground. There is something you must know; Mario switches between frames every tenth of a second no matter what you move left or right. Forget about the arrow keys. The reason, Mario defaults to his standard frame.

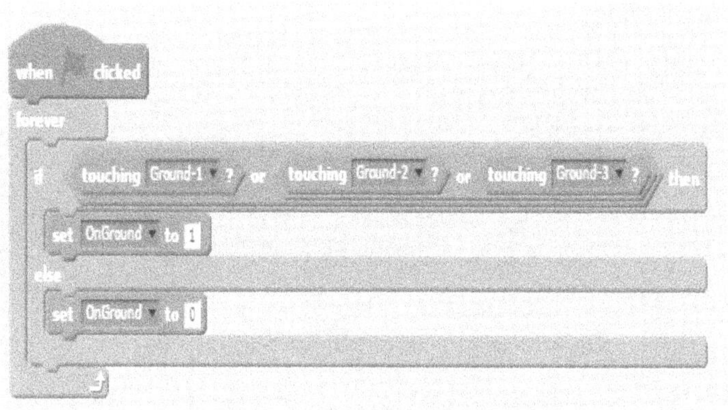

The onGround variable is not difficult to figure out. It can be done with a simple bit of code. In case that Mario touches one of the ground blocks, let's say OnGround equals 1 (true). In the other hand, i.e., when he's jumping, let's say the OnGround is 0 (false).

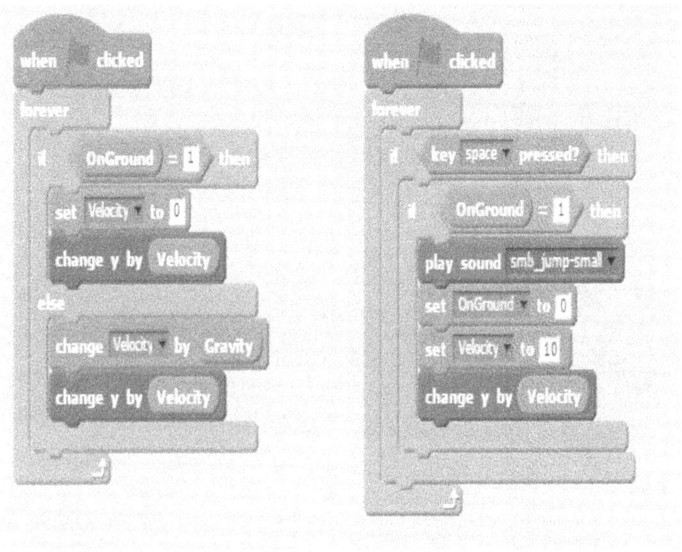

Mario's jump velocity is handled by the two blocks of code. On the left is a block that ensures Mario doesn't have any momentum if he's on the ground. If he's in the air, then his velocity is gradually slowed by gravity, which is a constant value. Whenever you click on the space bar, the right block makes Mario jump. It is important to note that speed drives Mario into the air. But that occurs until gravity takes over. However, before all that, the jump sound is played first.

```
when [flag] clicked
go to front
play sound 01-main-theme-overworld.mp3
set OnGround to 1
set Velocity to 0
set ScrollX to 0
set Gravity to -0.5
point in direction 90
go to x: 0 y: -115
```

Now, we can say that the last block of code for Mario is all setup. To start the music, click the green flag. All default values of all variables are set. Now, Mario is generated in the middle of the screen.

Collecting Coins

Let's jump back to the coins. One coin is disappeared and makes a sound when Mario grabs one. Let's make a separate script for that — separating scripts by function is an important practice in programming. A big jumble of blocks makes it harder to figure out the problem when something goes wrong.

Here's our coin collection script:

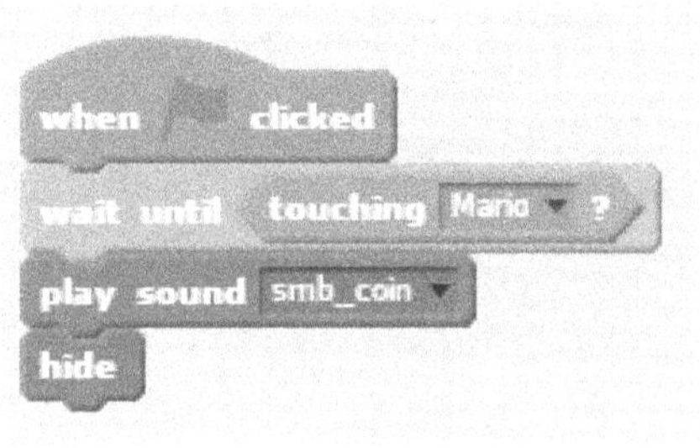

It's not difficult: It is important to note that the sound of the collection sounds and the currency is hidden when Mario touches him. Stop the coins reappear when the program restarts, a Show block is placed.

Scroll Coins and Clouds

You're almost there! Both coins and the ground must move while Mario is moving. So, Mario will be able to collect the coins:

```
when [flag] clicked
set y to (-60)
forever
  if <(ScrollX) > (0)> then
    set [ScrollX v] to (0)
  else
    set x to (((ScrollX) * (0.75)) + ((150) * (1)))
```

With this block Mario can grab the coin easily because it is placed the coin at a Y. To move towards Mario, similar ground logic can be used. So that the coins could move towards Mario, the speed has been increased to 0.75. However, the difficulty is increased when the set and field are increased to -40 and -20. That is, the coins are higher. It's going to be a little difficult for Mario to catch them. In the Set x to block, increase the 150 *1 to 150 *3 and 150 *5. This increasing if for 2nd and 3rd coins so that they can be placed further to the right, off-screen.

The clouds use a nearly identical block of code:

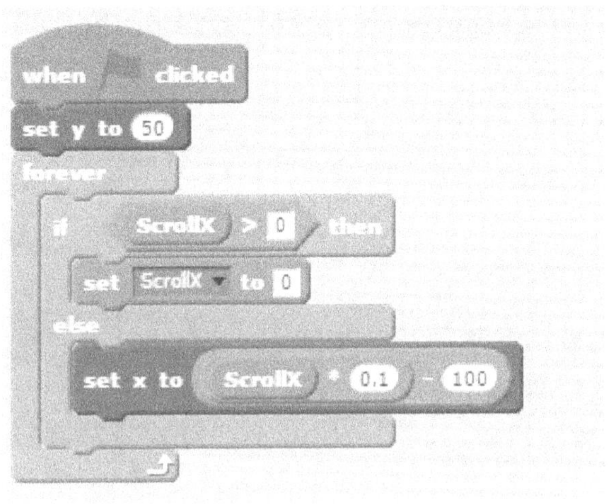

This code is to place a cloud at a specific height. When Mario is moving, it scrolls. For a second cloud that's in front of Mario instead of behind him, change the set x to block to (ScrollX * 0.1) + (150 * 1), just like the coins.

Add Borders

The coins are stuck on the edge of the screen. But they move towards the view. That is possible depending on the way you implement both the ground and the coins. This is unsightly, so you should create a quick border sprite that's the same color as the background to hide this on both the left and right sides.

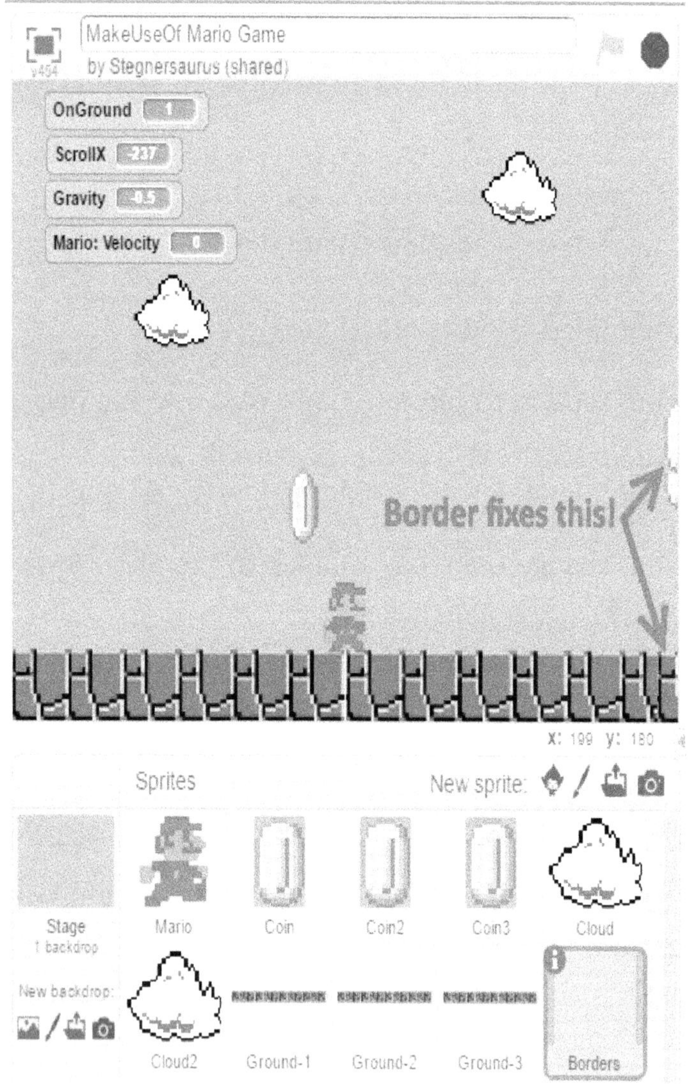

Go right there and make a right-click on the stage. Make a click on Save picture of stage. Open this in Paint.NET and use the pipette tool to select the blue background color. Add a new layer using the bottom-right dialogue. Then, use the rectangle tool to draw a filled blue rectangle on either side of the screen. Remove the background layer while covering half of each block.

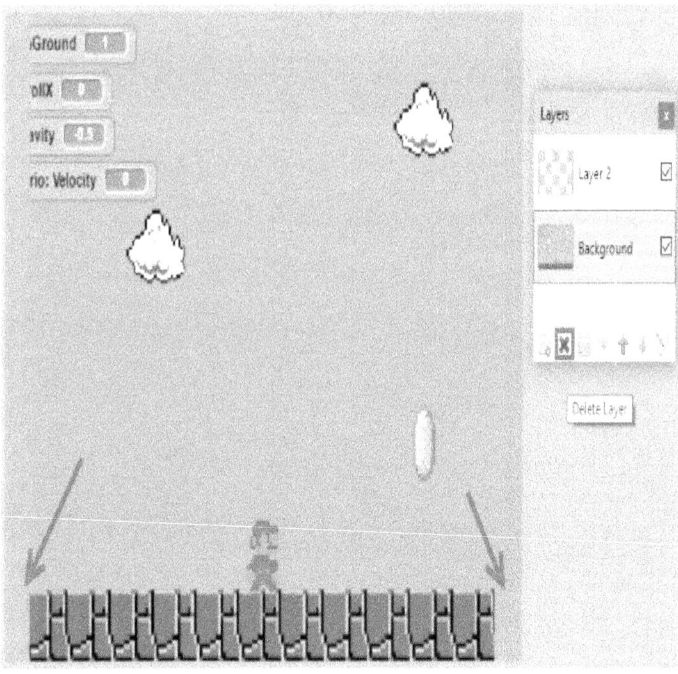

Upload it as a new sprite called border while you save it as a PNG file. Since you drew the borders right over the screen, you can line it up perfectly.

A few blocks that is needed so that the border is always in front.

```
when [flag] clicked
go to front
go to x: 0 y: -5
```

Scratch Games solutions

Game #1: Baby plays with a ball controlling by a player

This will be a game where the player will have full controls on a baby. In this game, we will use the arrow keys to catch a falling ball. In case that the baby misses the ball the game is over.

Start up Scratch

- Click on Scratch.exe

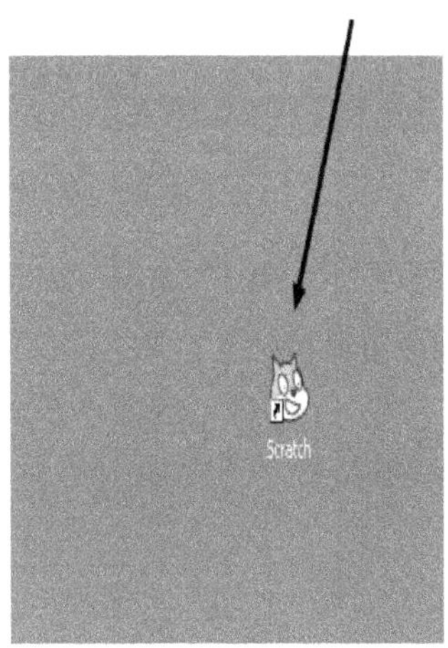

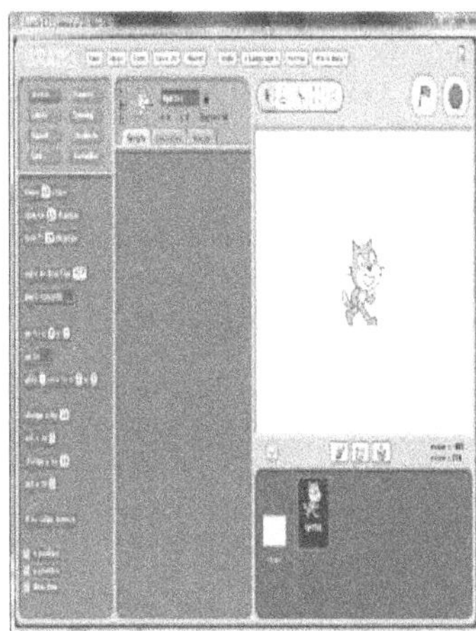

Delete the Cat

- Just make a click where is located thc scissors and your cursor turns to scissors and then click on the cat to delete it

- Or, to delete the cat, make right click on the cat choose delete

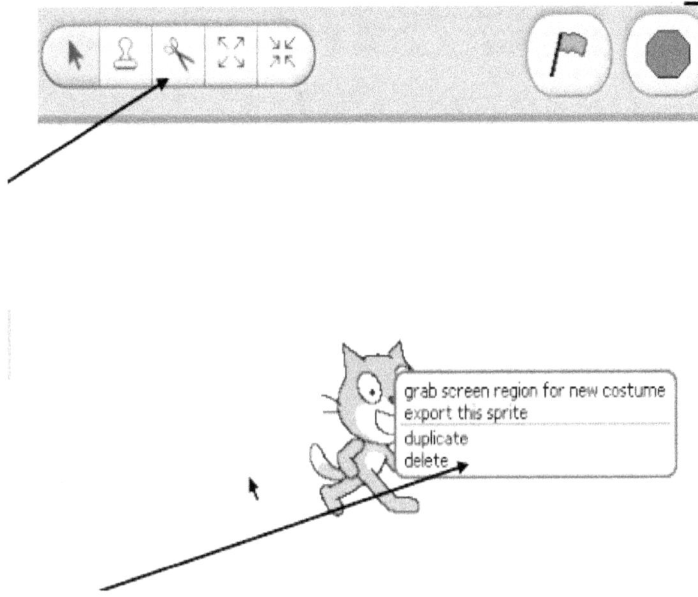

Add the Baby

Look for your picture to replace the cat previously deleted by clicking on the button with the picture of folder with a star in it-if you hover over it, it says "Choose new sprite from file"

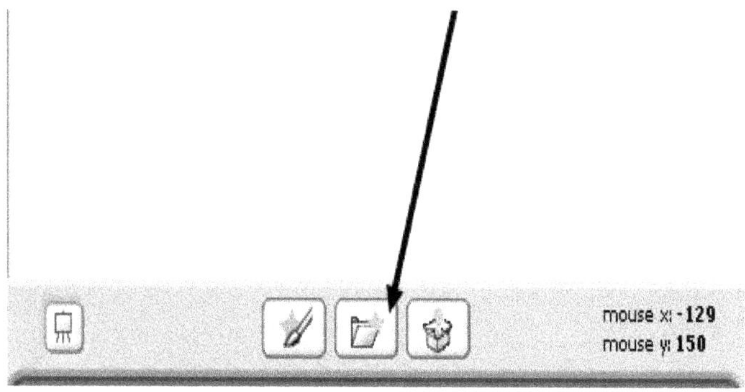

Select the People Folder

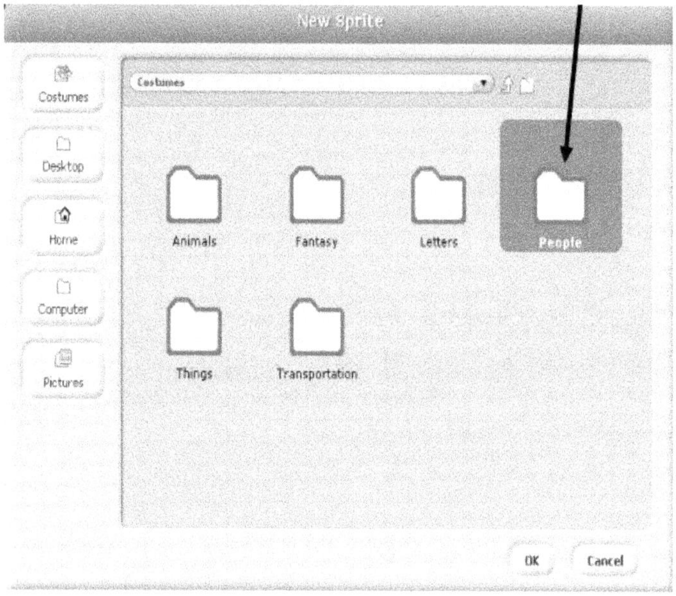

Scroll to the Baby

- Click on the baby and then OK

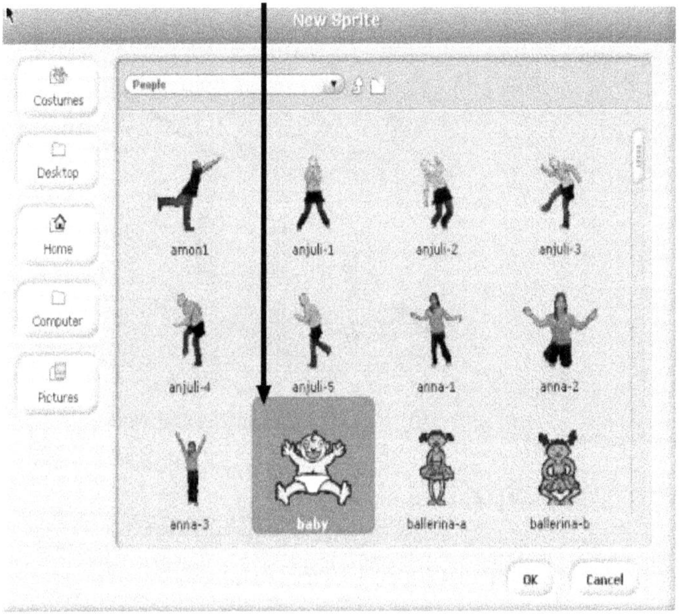

Change the size of your Sprite!

- .It depends on you to make your sprite larger or smaller by using the "grow sprite" or "shrink sprite" icons.
- Make a click on one of these icons, then choose your sprite until it is the size you'd

like.

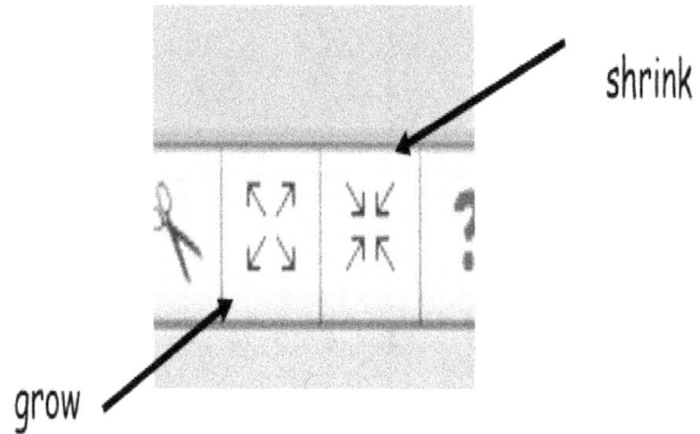

Move the Sprite

Move the sprite is easy, You must select the sprite. To do so, you must make a click on the arrow and then choose the sprite. After doing so, make a click in order to bring the sprite to the bottom of the window.

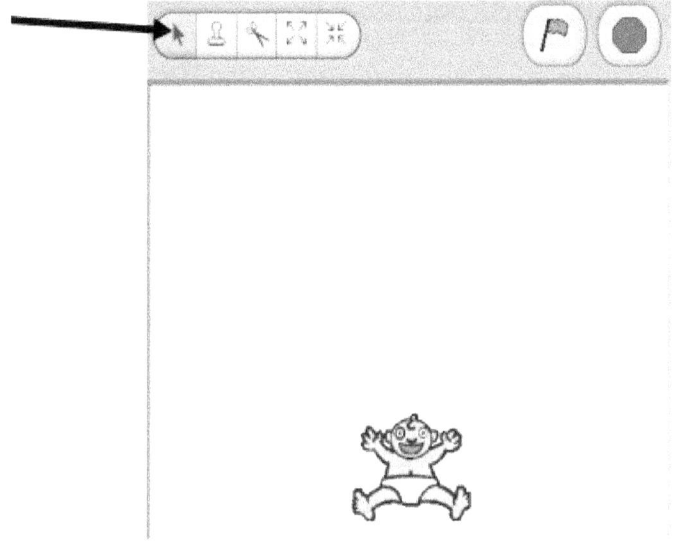

Add a Background

Click on the Stage

-In the right area, make a click in the button

- Make a click where is located the Backgrounds tab

- In the center

- Click on the import button
- Pick a background

- Like bedroom1 in indoors

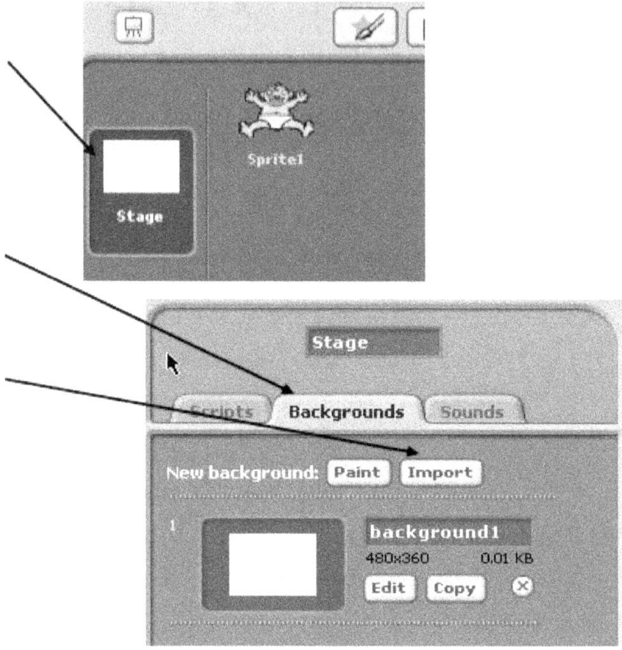

Now, it the time to add a Background To do so:

- Make a click on the Stage Event Handling
- In order to control the baby you must use the arrow keys

- When clicking the left arrow the baby will move left

- When clicking the right arrow the baby will move right

- We call this, a form of event handling

- To respond to user actions like mouse clicks and key presses The Scratch Stage

- 480 pixels wide and 360 pixels high are the scratch stage.

Moving left decreases the x value

Moving left decreases the

Moving right increases the x

180

-240

0,0

240

At the center of the stage

Programming the Baby

- In the view of the sprites and stage, make a click on the baby
  – Go right there on the Bottom right section

- Click on the Scripts tab

-In the center area

-This allows us to create scripts (programs) for the baby

-Each sprite can have several scripts

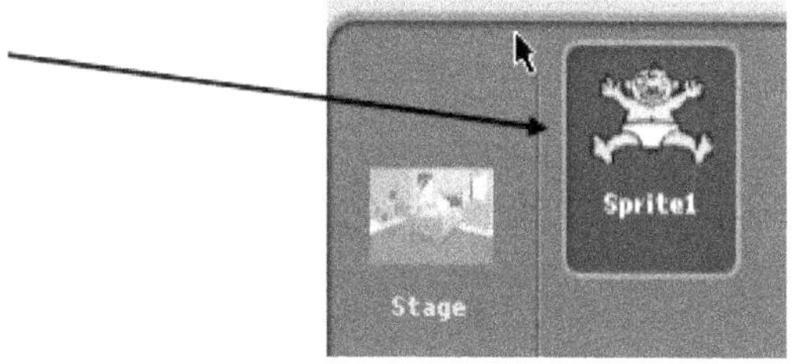

This area shows the current sprite

Respond to Arrow Keys

Make a click on Control, in the orange part. and then press the key of space to drag out.

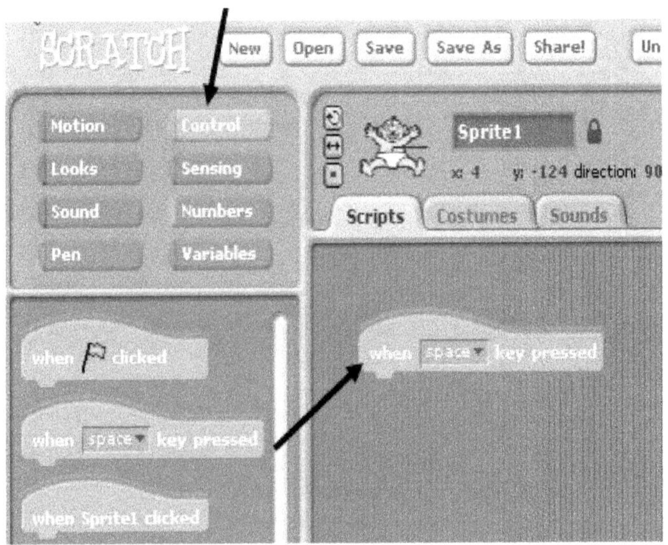

Respond to Right Arrow

- Make a click on down arrow near to space in order to select right arrow
- Make a click on Motion, where is located the blue part. and Bring to "move 10 steps"

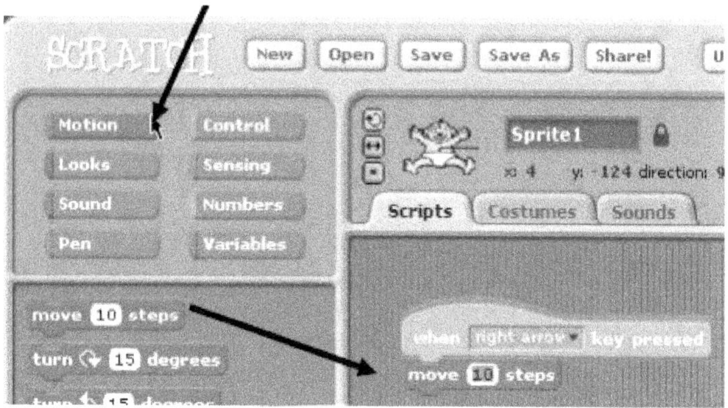

Let's change the move quantity

- Make a click where there are the 10

  - It will highlight in blue

- Type 5 and press enter

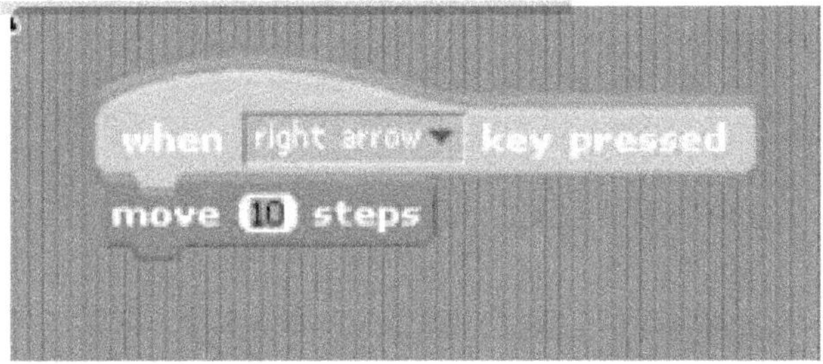

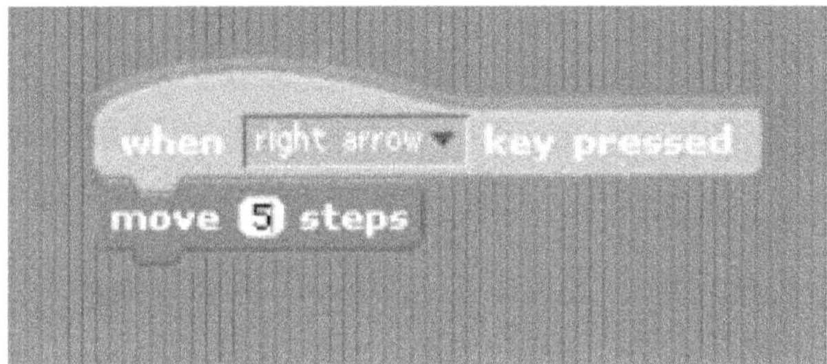

Respond to Arrow Keys

Click on Control (orange)

- Press the key space to Drag out
- Change "space" to "left arrow"
- Click on Motion
- Bring to "move 10 steps"
- Switch to -5, remember to move left

- Click on the stage and try outthe left and right arrow keys

  – Does the sprite leave the window?

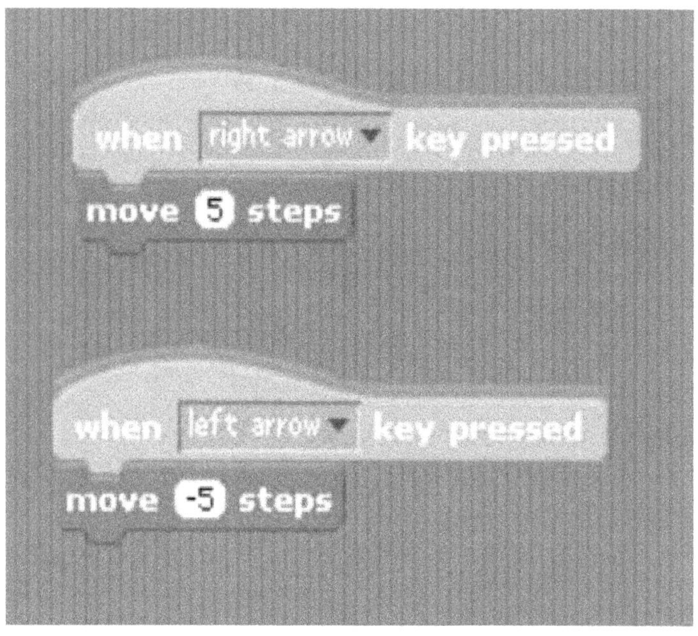

Paint a Ball

- Click on the brush and star

– The new message will be: "Paint new sprite" if you hover over key" it

Draw the Ball

Click the circle tool

– Then use the eyedropper to choose a color and then click in the drawing space and drag to form the ball

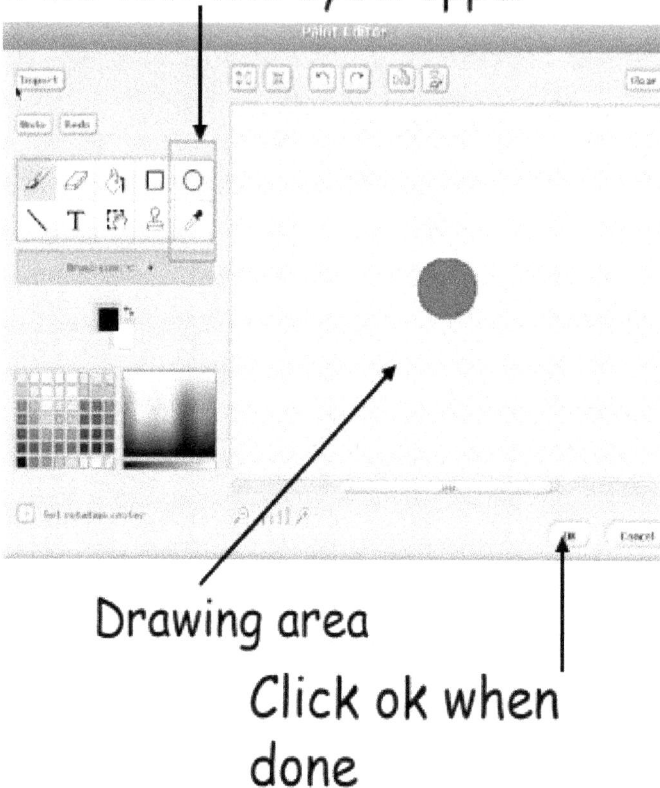

Make the size the ball in the way you want it to be. After doing so, you can move it to the top.

Make a click and drag the ball to the top of the window

Make the Ball Fall

- Once the green flag is clicked we want the ball to always start at the top and fall down

Make a click where it says management (orange)

– Drag out "When green flag clicked"

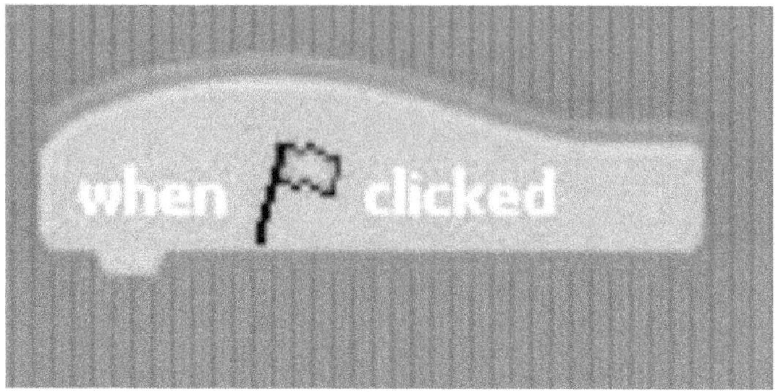

- Bring to "go to x # y #"

– This may perpetually begin the ball at its current position (Scratch doesn't automatically place it back for you).

Sequential Execution

For the block, one is executed after the other;

- This task is performed in order and from top to bottom
- When you make a click on the green flag

– The trajectory of the ball will be to the specified x and y location

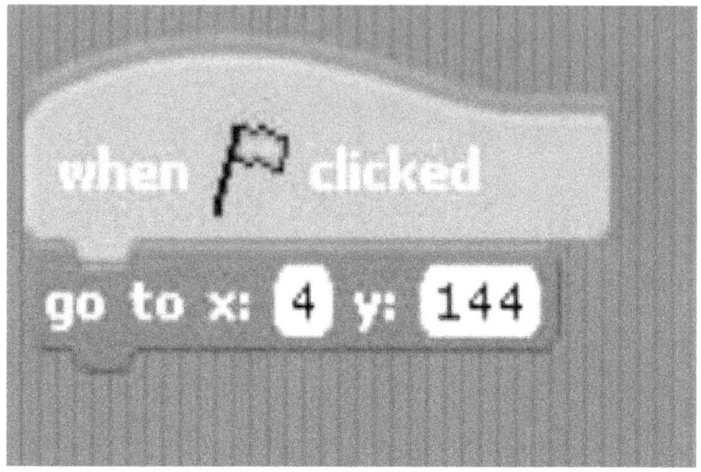

Loops

- Let's say that you want the ball to continue to move down unless the baby catches it
- How to do so?

– Lots of blocks could be used, one after the other

- However, it is not recommended since this would be slow and repetitive

- The most suitable is a way to repeat a block or set of blocks

- That's we called a loop or iteration.

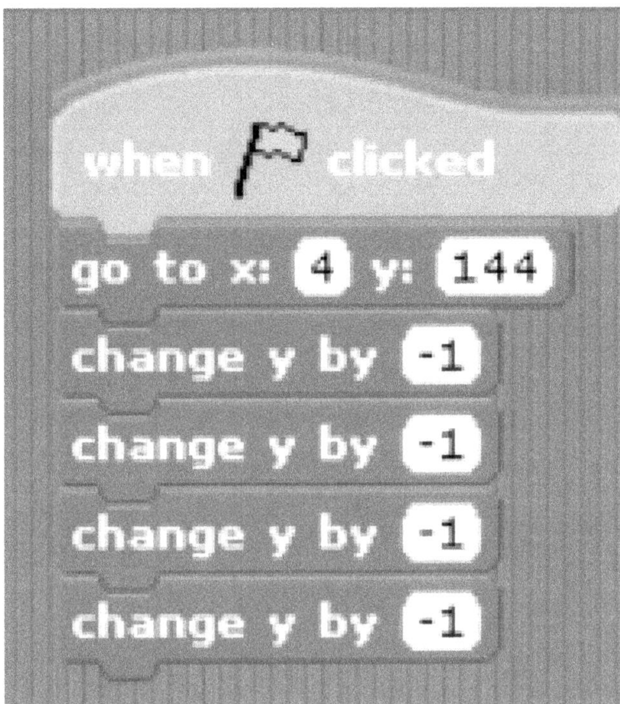

Now, let's make the ball fall

- Make a click on Management or Control, it is the orange part.

  – Bring to "forever"

- Make a click on Motion which is the blue part

– Bring to “switch y by 10”

– Switch it to -1

- Check it out!

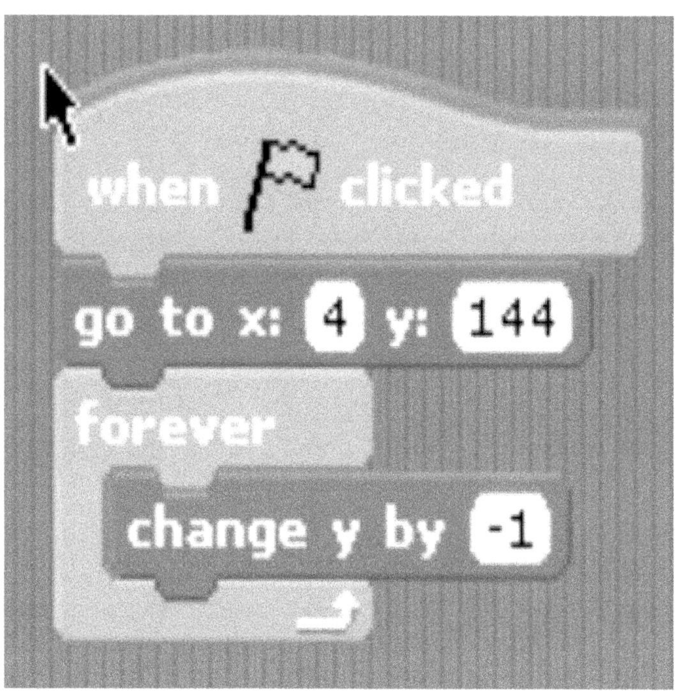

Catch the ball!

- If the ball touches the baby that means it is caught
- Why don't we try to track how many balls we have caught with a score?

– Let's increment the score each time we catch a ball

Variables

- In case that you are going to keep track of the score

– You want something to hold the current score

– And you want to change the score

– want the value to change or vary

- That's what we are called a variable

Track the score

- It is important to set the score to 0 when you start the game
- Make a click on Variables, which the red part
- Make a click on Make a Variable
- Give it the name Score

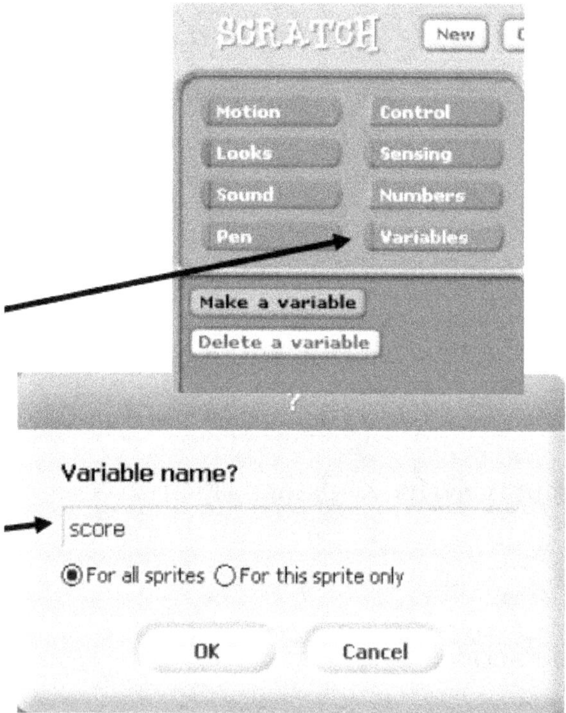

How to set score to 0?

- Go right there, In the ball script
- Bring to "forever"
- Bring to "set score to 0"
- Bring to "forever", backing up
- You will see the score in the window

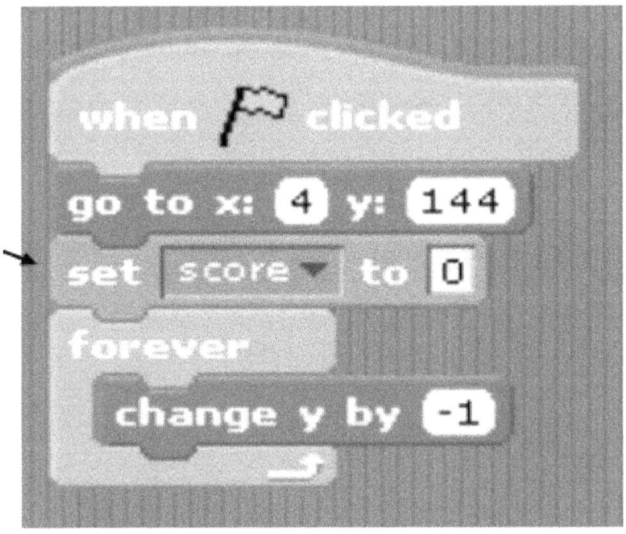

Conditionals

- In case that you want to increase the score if the baby caught the ball

–Be sure that this action will performed only if some condition is true

– That's what we call a conditional or an "if

Did the ball is caught?

- You must go on control, management in order to drag out an "if"

- Make sure that the ball touch the baby

– You can find this in Sensing

- In case that it is true, increase the score

–From Variables

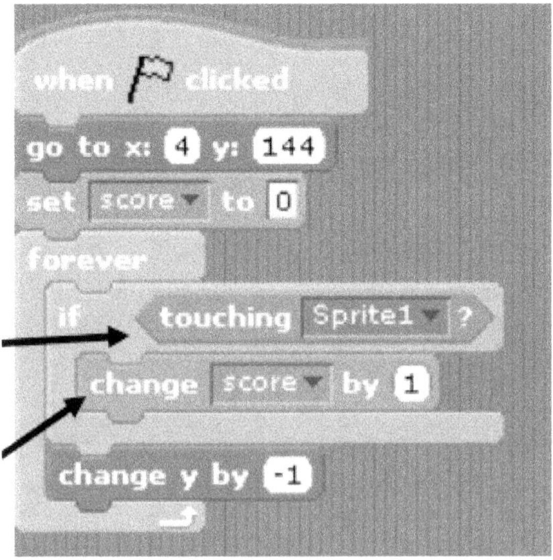

Increment the score

- Check it out!

  –Are you sure that is what you expected?

- You must have it clear that Computers execute what we command.

  – They don't execute what we want them to

How to reset the Ball?

- In case that the ball is caught

– You must increase the score

– You must move the ball to some random spot at the top of the window

– Don't keep incrementing the score

How to reset the Ball?

- Make a click on Number

 – Bring to "pick random 1 to 10"

 – Go right there on the x value after "go to x:"

 – Switch the 1 to -235 and switch 10 to 235

 – Switch the y value in order to match the y in the first "go to x # y #

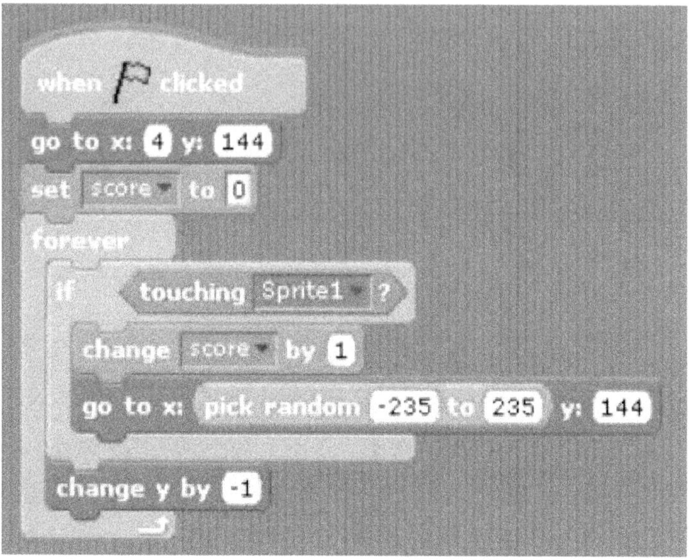

How to add Losing?

- In case that the baby doesn't catch the ball, it because of it gets stuck at the bottom of the screen
- Now, how to tell the player that he lost?

To add a text sprite:

- You must make a click on the Paint new sprite button

  – Make click on the T for text

– Choose the color

– If you want to modify the font size, you can do so.

– Change the square the direction to where you want the text

– Write: You Lost!

How to hide the sprite?

- It doesn't make sense tell the player that she lost when the game starts

– The best thing you can do is to hide the message when the game starts. To do so:

- Make a click on Control or management

– Bring to "when green flag clicked"

- Make a click on Looks

– Bring to "hide"

Now, let's check if lost

- In case that the y position gets near the bottom, that is, near -180

  – Write an "if"

- From Control

  – bring to a blank < blank

- From Numbers

  – put in a y position

- From Motion

  – Write in -175

How to broadcast a message?

- You can communicate the Sprites only by passing messages

– One of them broadcasts the message

– The others can listen for the first one and react to it when they receive it

– Make a click on Control

- Bring to "broadcast blank"
- Make a click on the drop down arrow next to new

–Give it the name lost

- put a “stop script”

– This, to stop the forever loop

How to receive Lost?

- Make click on the text sprite
- Make a click on Control

– Bring to "when I receive blank"

– Make a click on the down arrow and choose lost

- Make a click on Looks

– Bring to “show”

- Make a click on Control

– Bring to “stop all”

- This, to stop all scripts

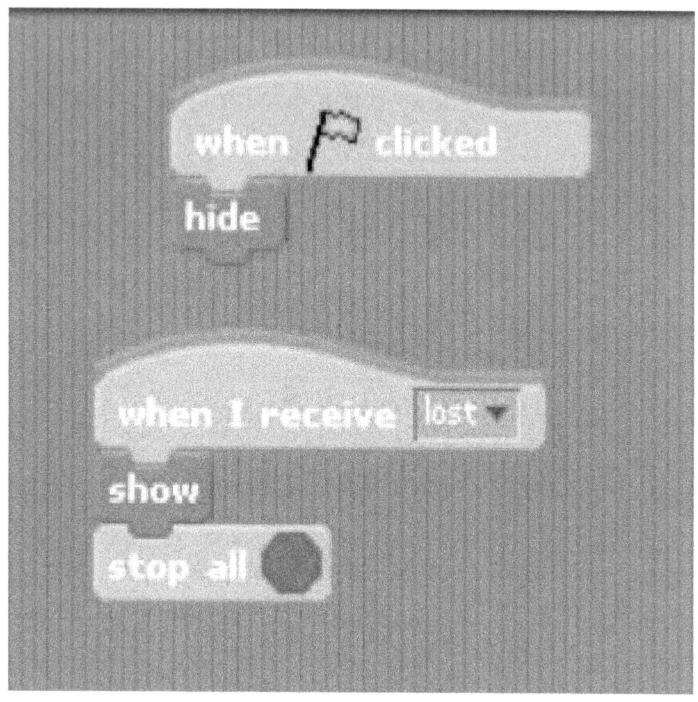

What is parallel Execution?

- There are a lot of things that happening at the same time

  – When clicking the green flag

- We call this action parallel execution

-It is impossible to say only one thing is happening.

How to create Instructions?

- Make a click on the Show Project Notes icon in the upper right corner
- Put the instructions
- Click OK

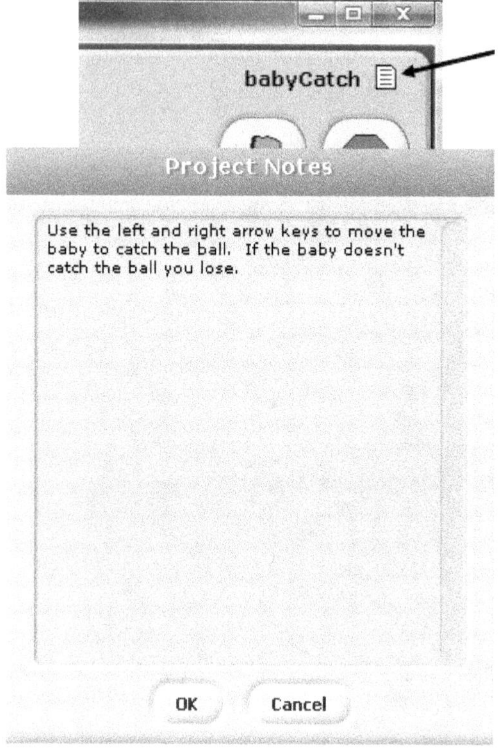

You must test your game, to do so:

- Make a click in the green flag
- Adjust the speed of the ball (optional)

  – Increment the quantity it switches in y
- Change the sprites by using the "Costume" tab

- You must save your game by clicking the "Save" button

How to share your game?

- When you make sure that everything is ok, it's time to share your projects at the scratch web site
- Make a click on the Share! button

Other Ideas

- You can put sound when player loses
- Put the ability to win

– When they player reaches an amount of score

– You can also track the amount of time it takes as well

- You can even speed up the ball over time
- You can put more sprites to catch

Conclusion

We have seen programming in scratch is not difficult. There is no doubt that it is because Scratch is a visual programming language designed for children from 6-8 years. Scratch allows easily creating games, animations and telling stories, joining blocks to form the instructions of the program. It means you can learn how the code is structured and what it does without the frustration of having to learn the syntax and get started quickly.

It does not require prior knowledge of computer science, beyond the use of the mouse, copy/paste and have ever used a web browser.

It is also very fun to use and has a huge community of users whose projects you can see and copy, which helps you learn practically.

In this eBook, you have learned about how Scratch works and the main components of a Scratch project. If you practice what we have put in this eBook, you will learn how to use all these components to create your projects, stage, and sprites.

www.ingramcontent.com/pod-product-compliance
Lightning Source LLC
LaVergne TN
LVHW022314060326
832902LV00020B/3450

* 9 7 8 1 9 9 0 0 5 9 9 5 7 *